21st Century Houses Downunder

21st Century Houses
Downunder

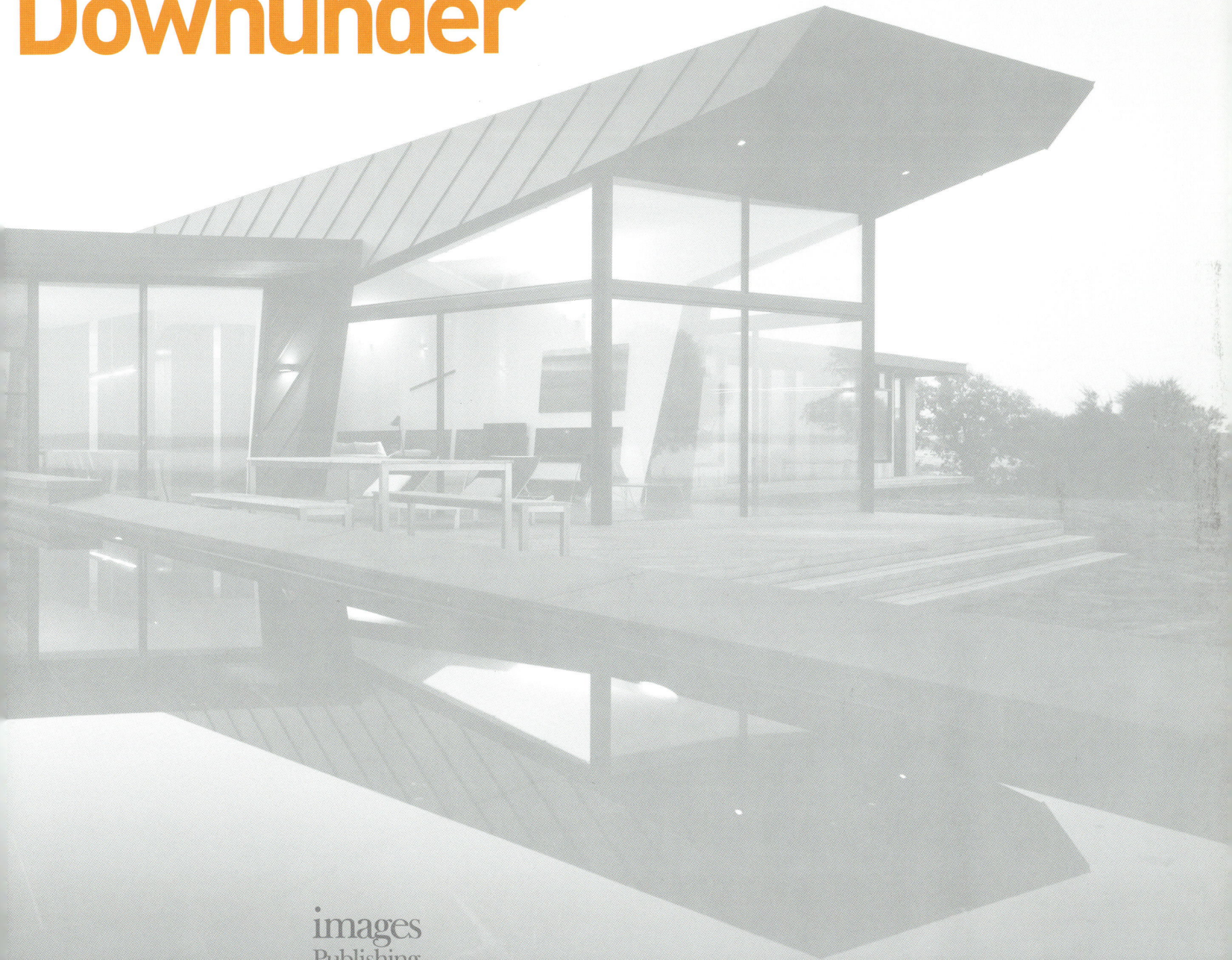

images
Publishing

Published in Australia in 2010 by

The Images Publishing Group Pty Ltd

ABN 89 059 734 431

6 Bastow Place, Mulgrave, Victoria 3170, Australia

Tel: +61 3 9561 5544 Fax: +61 3 9561 4860

books@imagespublishing.com

www.imagespublishing.com

National Library of Australia Cataloguing-in-Publication entry

Title:	21st century houses downunder / edited by Mark Cleary.
ISBN:	9781864704204
Series:	21st century.
Notes:	Includes index.
Subjects:	Architecture – Australia – History – 21st century.
	Architecture – New Zealand – History – 21st century.
	Interior decoration – Australia – History – 21st century.
	Interior decoration – New Zealand – History – 21st century.
	Architecture – Australia – Designs and plans.
	Architecture – New Zealand – Designs and plans.

Other Authors/Contributors: Cleary, Mark.

Dewey Number: 720.994

Designed by The Graphic Image Studio Pty Ltd, Mulgrave, Australia

www.tgis.com.au

Pre-publishing services by United Graphic Pte Ltd, Singapore

Printed on 150 gsm Quatro Silk Matt paper by Everbest Printing Co. Ltd., in Hong Kong/China

IMAGES has included on its website a page for special notices in relation to this and our other publications. Please visit www.imagespublishing.com.

Pages 2-3: Beached House by BKK Architects; photography by Peter Bennetts

Page 6: Balhannah House by Max Pritchard Architect; photography by Sam Noonan

Page 263: Carlton House by Nic Owen Architects; photography by Rhiannon Slatter

Contents

070 Residence

Indooroopilly, Queensland, Australia

Push

Photography: Clare and Papi

The 070 Residence is set on an expansive site with south-facing river frontage and a dramatic 30-metre elevational drop to the tidal zone. The plan diagram seeks to integrate the river aspect setting with usable north-facing outdoor living and safe play areas.

The design resolves itself as a classic courtyard home with a two-storey L-shaped volume and a separated single-level guest wing framing the double-height court. The courtyard is penetrated by openings to the north, under and through the high-level fretted screen, and to the east between the buildings to the pool. The change in scale of fenestration, solid building masses and opening voids creates the spatial variations evident in classical courtyard design. This is the nucleus of the family house, spatially and visually connecting the common living and landscape play areas from a single central position.

Orientated to the north–east to take full advantage of passive environmental benefits, seasonal sun control is controlled by a fixed louvre screen that creates a visible statement to the street front and defines the court as the entry threshold for the house.

1 Kitchen
2 Deck
3 Pool
4 Lounge
5 Dining room
6 Guest bedroom
7 Ensuite
8 Study
9 Bedroom
10 Sitting room

First floor

0   5m

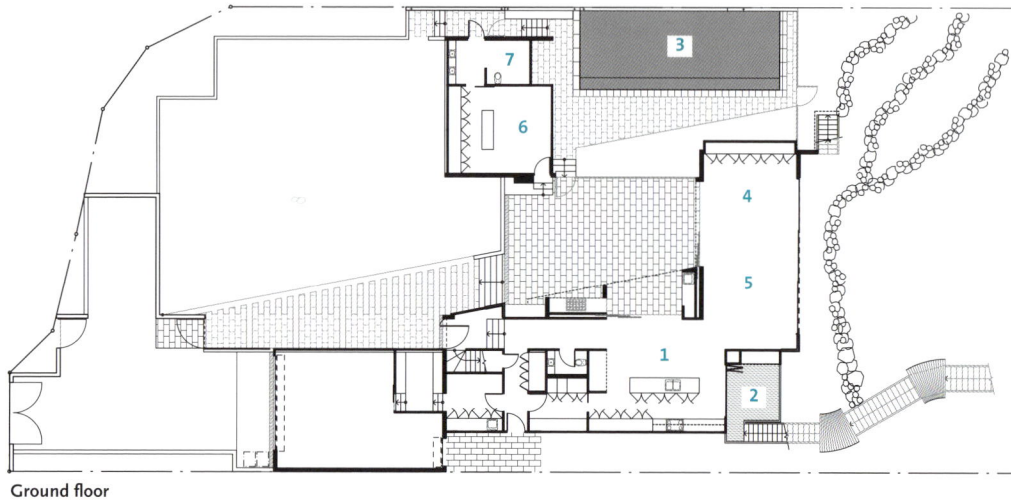

Ground floor

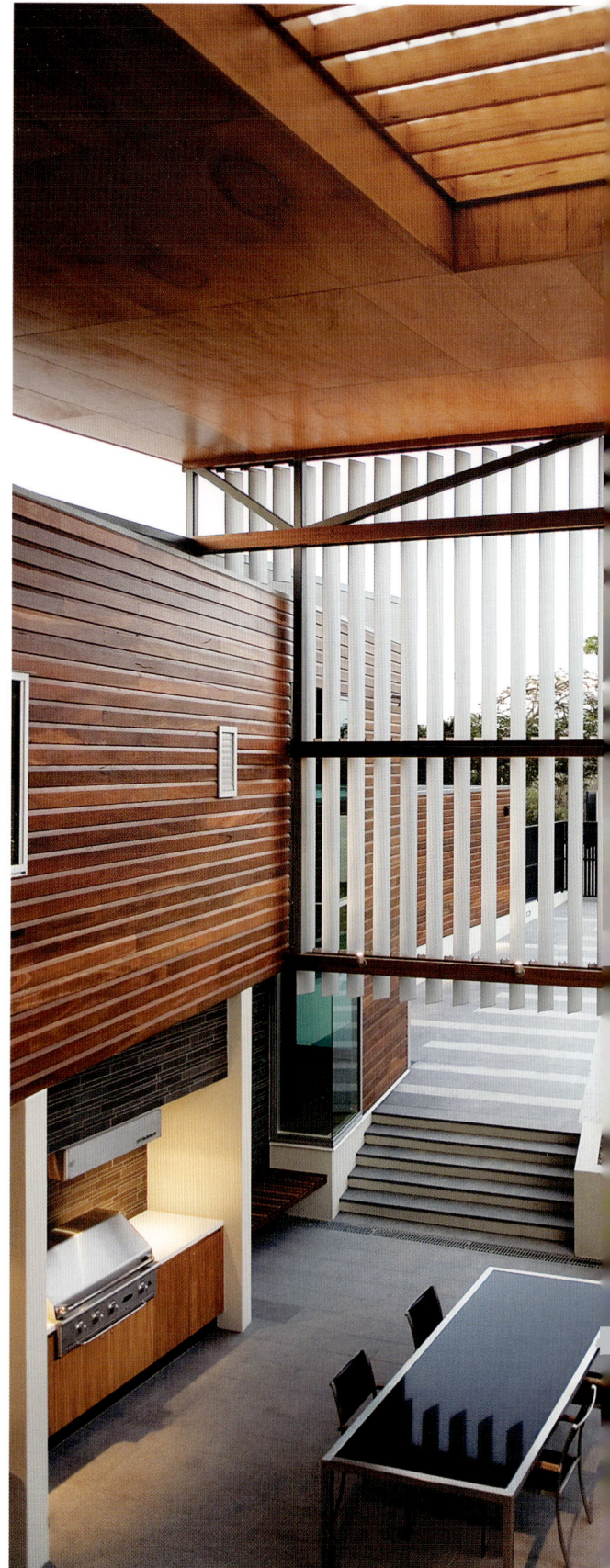

Elevation

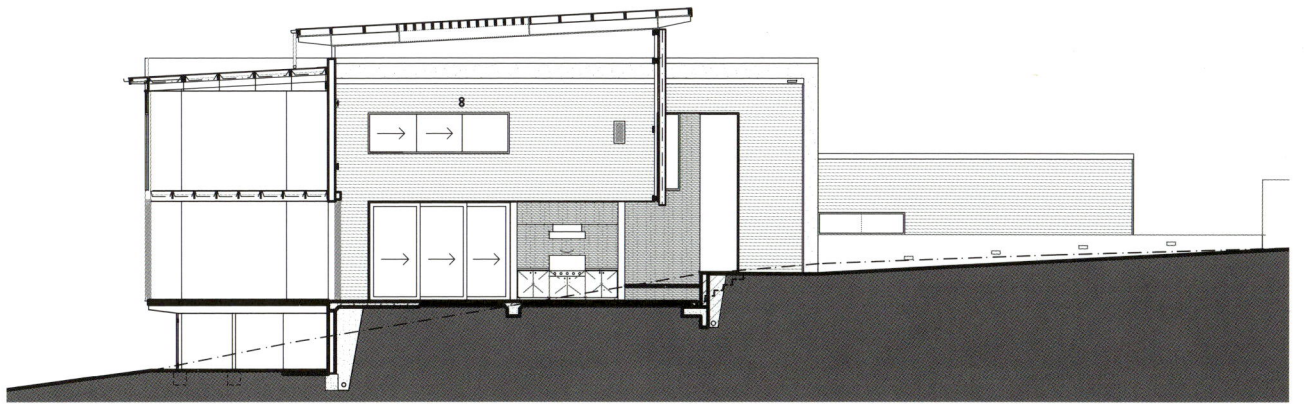

Acton House

Acton Park, Tasmania, Australia

Preston Lane Architects

Photography: Jonathan Wherrett

Acton House is located at the rear of a broad acre rural property in the heart of Acton Park. Access to the site is via a long internal driveway from the east, which makes its way along the northern boundary before coming across the face of existing horse stables near the entry of the house. From here the level splits to establish separation between the main house and work areas of the property.

The plan is configured as four wings—one for living, one for master sleeping, one for guest sleeping, with the final wing having close access to the stables. All are connected by a central entry space.

Masonry walls line the rear edges of each wing, reinforcing the directional nature of the building and providing privacy from the adjacent parts. The 'living' wing is located on the most eastern edge of the house, opening onto a courtyard area along its northern edge, providing maximum solar gain and shelter from the prevailing winds. An additional deck is accessed from the study space overlooking the courtyard and provides a shaded area for relaxing and surveying the site.

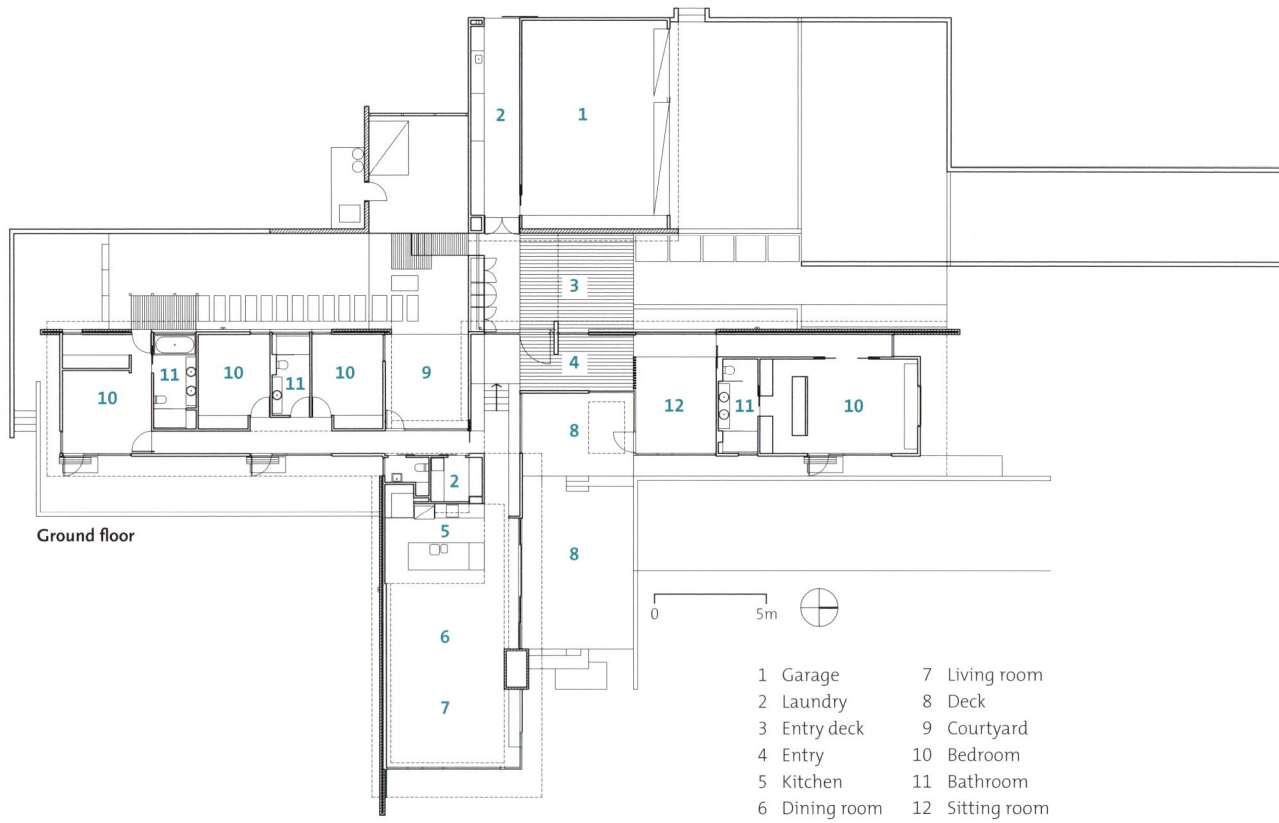

Ground floor

0   5m

1	Garage	7	Living room
2	Laundry	8	Deck
3	Entry deck	9	Courtyard
4	Entry	10	Bedroom
5	Kitchen	11	Bathroom
6	Dining room	12	Sitting room

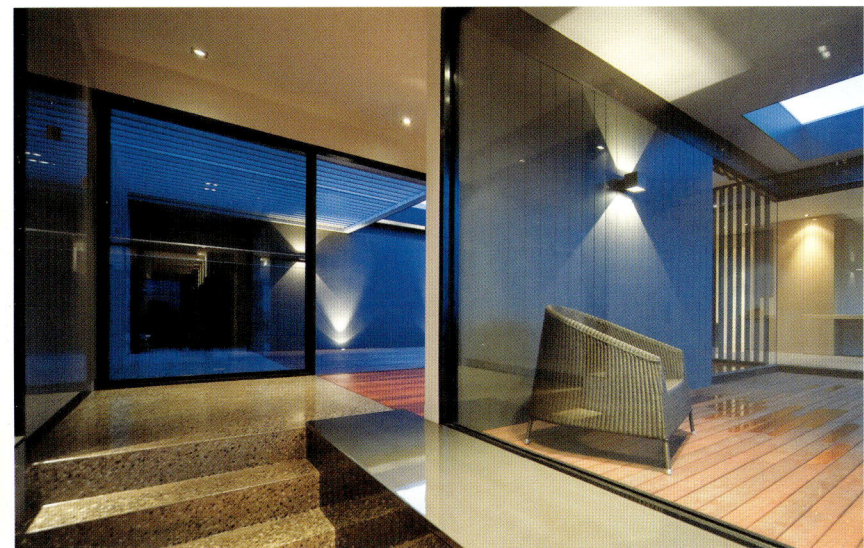

Annandale House

Annandale, NSW, Australia

Tobias Partners

Photography: Justin Alexander

This residence, located in Sydney's inner-west, was one of many single-storey Federation terraces in the area that make up the charming low-level streetscapes.

The initial client brief was simply to dramatically improve the living potentials of a small run-down house on a long, narrow plot. From this, two key challenges arose—how to create generous spaces throughout, while ensuring the building interior never felt too deep, dark or narrow; and how to keep the scale of the building modest, and ensure that the potential three storeys never appeared as one solid volume.

The existing terrace was retained and reworked at the front. The scheme plays with different volumes—some overhanging others, some double-height—from a raised deck area over the garage at the rear, up to the master bedroom at the top, which commands views over the neighbourhood to the city.

The front section of the house is separated from the rear by a semi-internal courtyard. This crucial space allows light to filter in and is viewed from many of the internal spaces. The scheme maximises all the potential on this fairly tight site, yet the building still sits within the scale of the surrounding context.

Ground floor

First floor

1 Entry
2 Bedroom
3 Bathroom
4 Study/Bedroom
5 Semi-internal courtyard
6 Dining room
7 Kitchen

8 Living room
9 Rear courtyard
10 Raised deck with garage under
11 Through to garage and laundry
12 Walk-in-robe
13 Balcony

0   4m

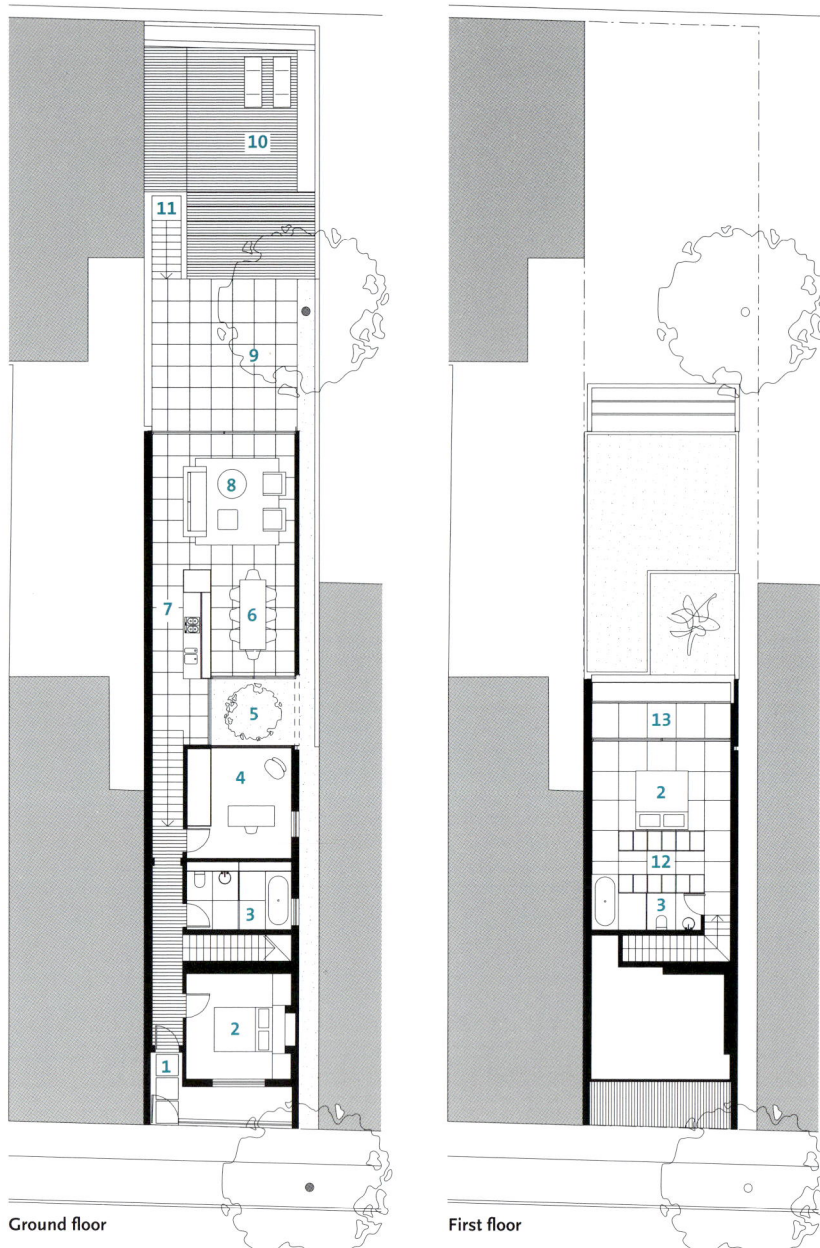

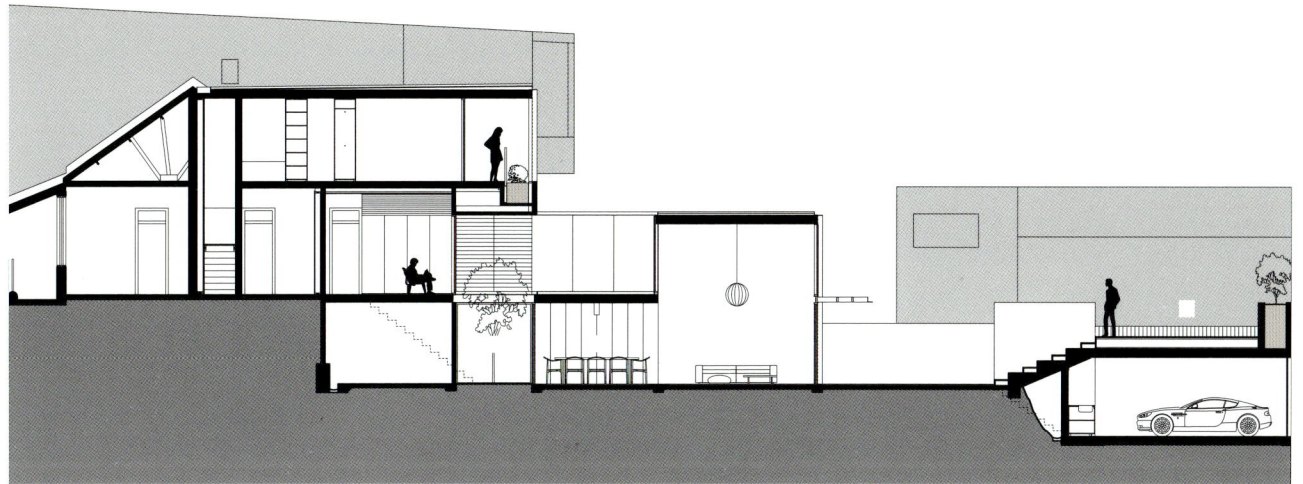

Elevation

Arbour House

New Farm, Brisbane, Australia

Richard Kirk Architect

Photography: Scott Burrows
(Aperture Photography)

Arbour House, located on the Bulimba Reach of the Brisbane River, is a study in siting and intricate articulation to yield views and landscape connections.

The long, thin 13-metre-wide site is located between two key public spaces—an established historic arbour of fig trees and a public riverfront boardwalk. The site, which once formed part of the surrounding multi-residential enclave, is now distinguished by a new single detached dwelling. Unlike other riverfront houses, the new dwelling is sited a respectful distance from the river's edge, preserving an 80-year-old Poinciana tree and historic public views from the boardwalk of the adjoining heritage-listed dwelling.

The large setback creates a platform for a private garden under the shade of the canopy of the Poinciana tree. The level of the platform and the height of the Poinciana tree and the arbour established the two datums for the setout of public and private spaces of the dwelling. The public riverfront living levels are adjacent to this space while the rear living spaces are elevated above the garage to look into the canopy of the arbor. The private bedroom spaces of the upper level are raised to a height to afford views of the tree canopy and river, yet offering privacy from the public river boardwalk.

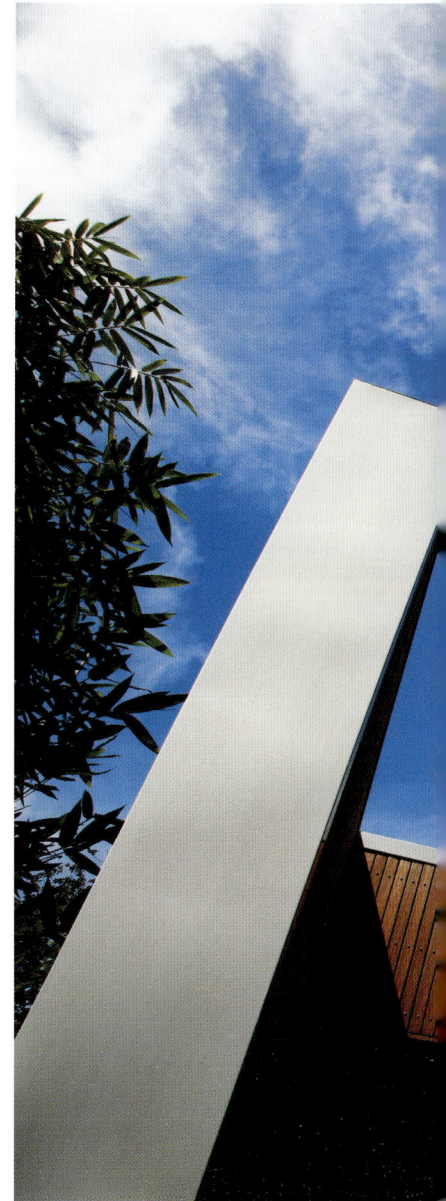

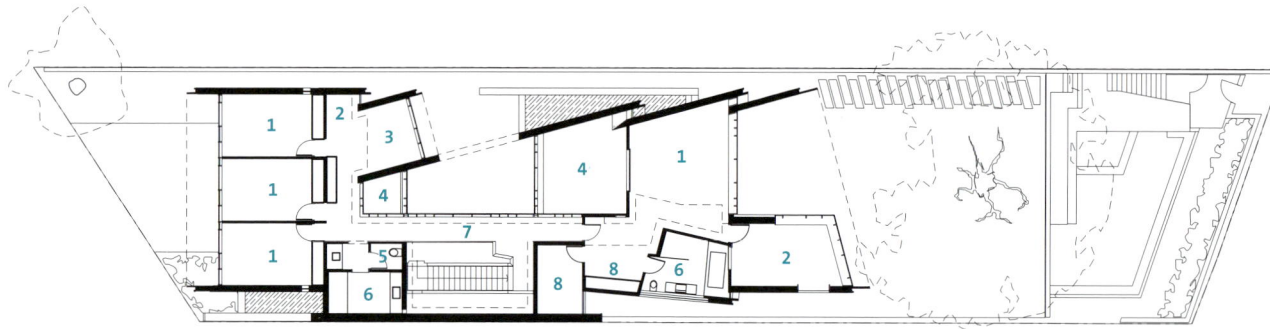

First floor

1 Bedroom
2 Study
3 Play area
4 Void
5 Powder room
6 Bathroom
7 Bridge
8 Robe

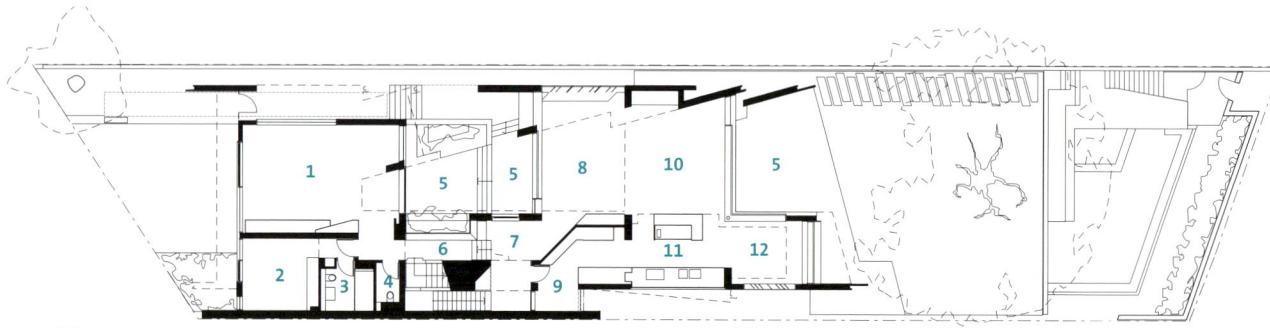

Ground floor

1 Family room
2 Bedroom
3 Bathroom
4 Powder room
5 Terrace
6 Hall
7 Entry
8 Dining room
9 Study
10 Living room
11 Kitchen
12 Meals area

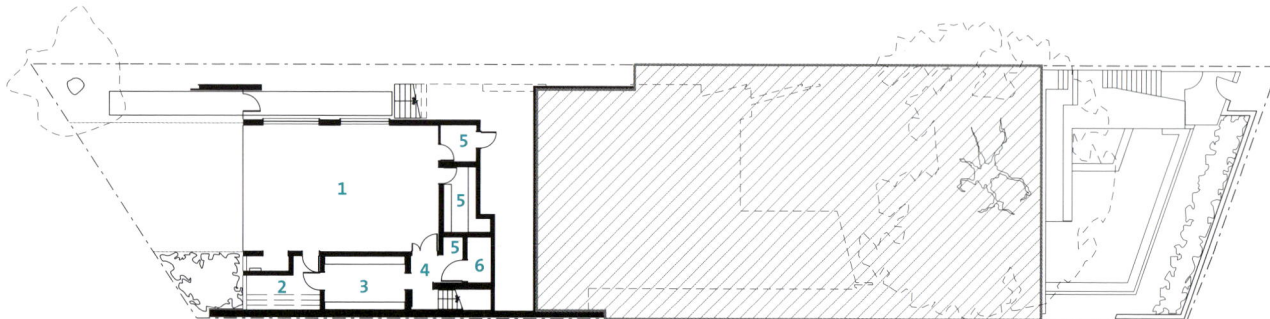

Basement

1 Garage
2 Drying court
3 Laundry
4 Hall
5 Store room
6 Cellar

0 _____ 5m

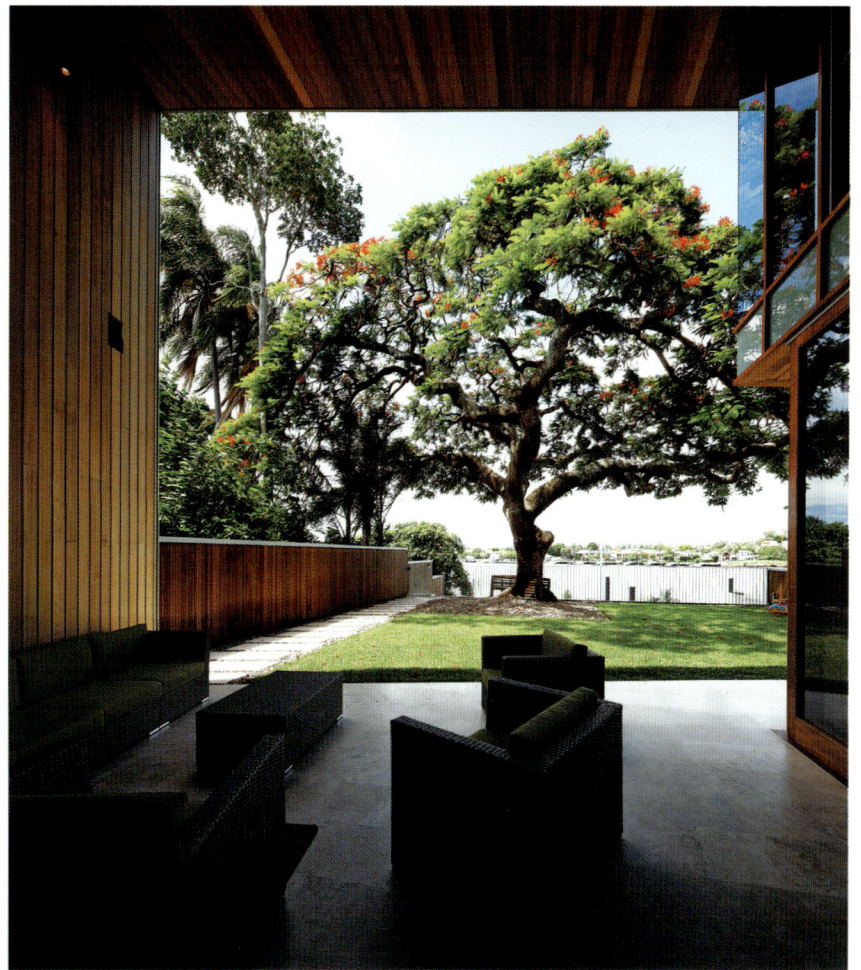

Balhannah House

Balhannah, South Australia, Australia

Max Pritchard Architect

Photography: Sam Noonan

Balhannah House is set before a backdrop of large gum trees with views over rolling hills of pasture and vineyards. The owners required a large home, but one that employed sound environmental principles, including passive thermal design, water collection and solar panels, as well as integrating into the beautiful rural site.

The long, thin form follows the site contours, minimising earthworks and maximising solar orientation and views. A strong element is the floating skillion roofs, following the ground slope. Corrugated iron and stone walls are traditional rural materials used effectively in a modern context.

The house's north-facing position maximises exposure to the sun for winter heating, while the external louvres over the terrace may be adjusted for summer shade. Photovoltaic cells on the roof generate electricity, and incorporate a unique feature allowing excess heat to be ducted down to the house to aid winter heating. Roof water is collected in a large underground tank, for use throughout the house. Timber, corrugated iron, stone and weathered steel provide a timeless rural quality in a contemporary style.

Although a substantial home, Balhannah House acts as a model in demonstrating sound environmental principles, using forms and materials appropriate to the context.

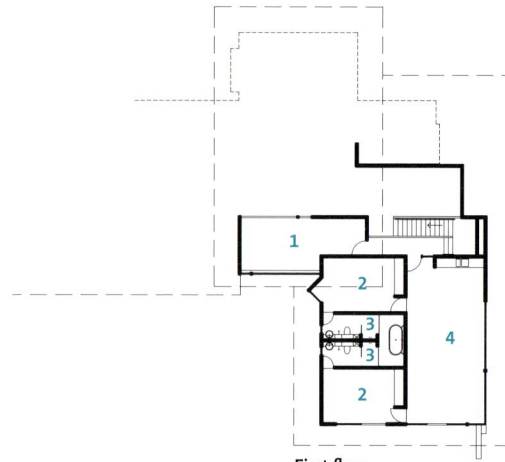

First floor

1 Study
2 Bedroom
3 Ensuite
4 Rumpus room

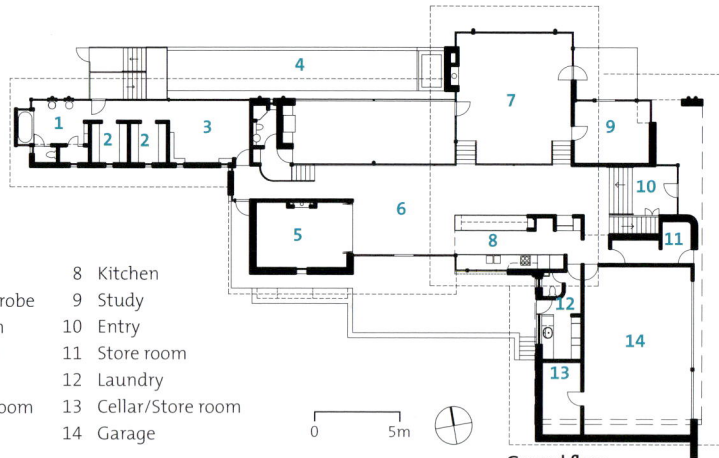

Ground floor

1 Ensuite
2 Walk-in-robe
3 Bedroom
4 Lap pool
5 Theatre
6 Dining room
7 Lounge

8 Kitchen
9 Study
10 Entry
11 Store room
12 Laundry
13 Cellar/Store room
14 Garage

0   5m

Balmoral House

Balmoral, Queensland, Australia

Arkhefield

Photography: Scott Burrows
(Aperture Photography)

Balmoral House is an overtly contemporary pavilion extension to an existing Queensland cottage in one of Brisbane's inner-city suburbs. The colour, material and form of the house deliberately contrast the new and old elements in a complementary manner.

The outdoor spaces are captured within the bounds of the house, with the courtyard between old and new forming a new gathering place, opening to the north and linked to the adjacent kitchen, becoming the centre of a new household.

The living room is light-filled and positioned to take in views of the city over the top of the existing house. Above this is perched the parents' bedroom, secluded for privacy but engaged through overlooking the central outdoor space. It is a captured landscape, structured for contemplation, and related directly to the new living room.

From the front of the house, new slender silver-weathered tallowwood screening contrasts against the regimented painted timber weatherboards. In the central courtyard, black-painted vertical groove plywood distinguishes the new extension from the traditional horizontal grey weatherboards of the existing house. Internally, the kitchen's new Tasmanian oak joinery is offset against the dark timbers of the heritage home. VJ panelling, decorative mouldings and the expressed structure of the Queenslander morph into the smooth, clean walls, shadow lines and square edges of the extension. What was once introverted and dark has now become extroverted and light.

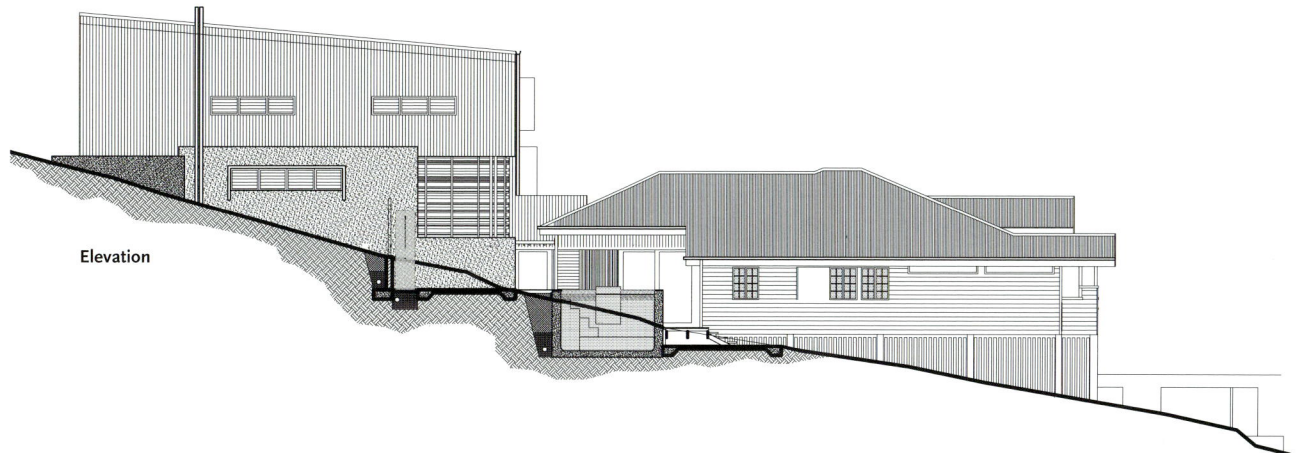

Elevation

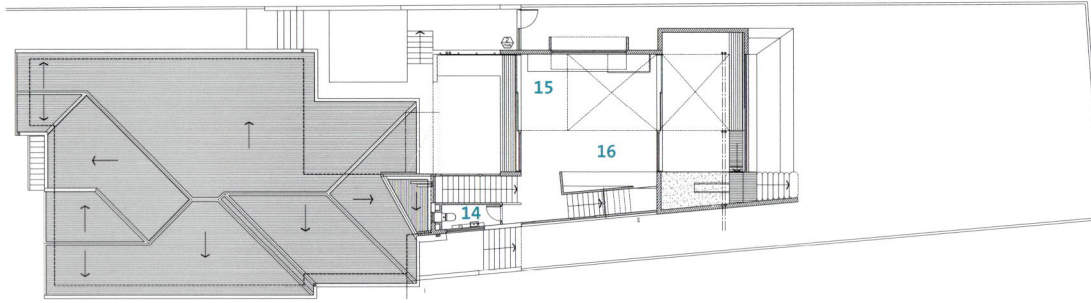

First floor

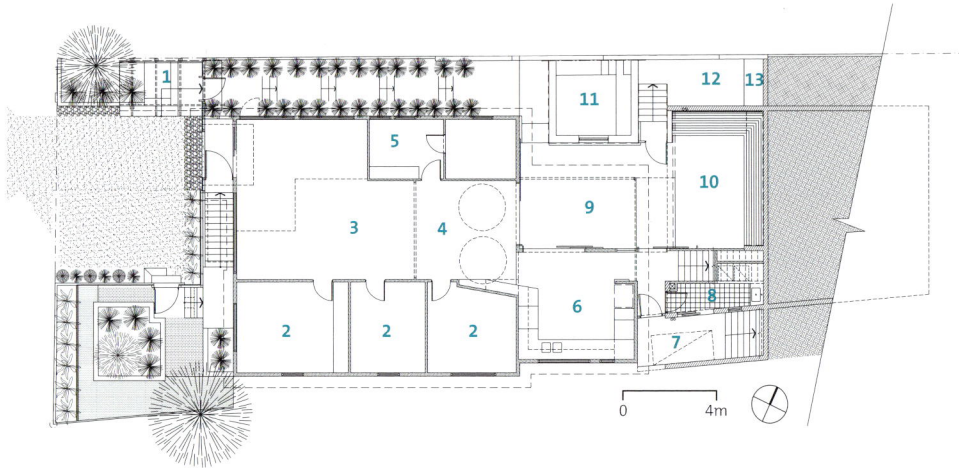

Ground floor

1 Front entrance gate
2 Bedroom
3 Living area
4 Dining room
5 Study
6 Kitchen
7 Drying court
8 Laundry
9 Courtyard
10 Outdoor living area
11 Pool
12 Pool deck
13 Outdoor shower
14 Powder room
15 Family room
16 Kitchenette

0 4m

Balquhidder

Nelson, South Island, New Zealand

Irving Smith Jack Architects

Photography: John-Paul Pochin
Photography

Balquhidder is a vineyard located on the Waimea River plain near Nelson. The alluvial land is flat, with a river border. Mindful of the need for flexibility in the best future utilisation of their land, the owners sought a small home that could be capable of removal or relocation should circumstances dictate, as well as making the most of the location, taking in the rural views and providing outdoor living.

A simple, low form was appropriate to the broad rural landscape. Basically one-room wide, the house runs north–south, with a broad protective eave along the east side. To the west, the roof falls low and changes in pitch to encompass the carport. Extending walls anchor the house to the ground.

Within the linear footprint, master and guest facilities occupy opposite ends, separated by a central living space that opens both sides to flanking decks and surrounding views. The elevated outlook gives a mid-ground to the views and reveals the receding patterns of vines, changing with the seasons. Decks provide outdoor living choices that respond to the sun and opposing winds.

Internal spaces are enlarged through simple volumes, generous daylight, a rising ceiling, sideways expansion to the decks, and an end-to-end view glimpse along the spine. Materials are wood and neutral plasterboard, with the form articulated inside and out by sparing use of colour.

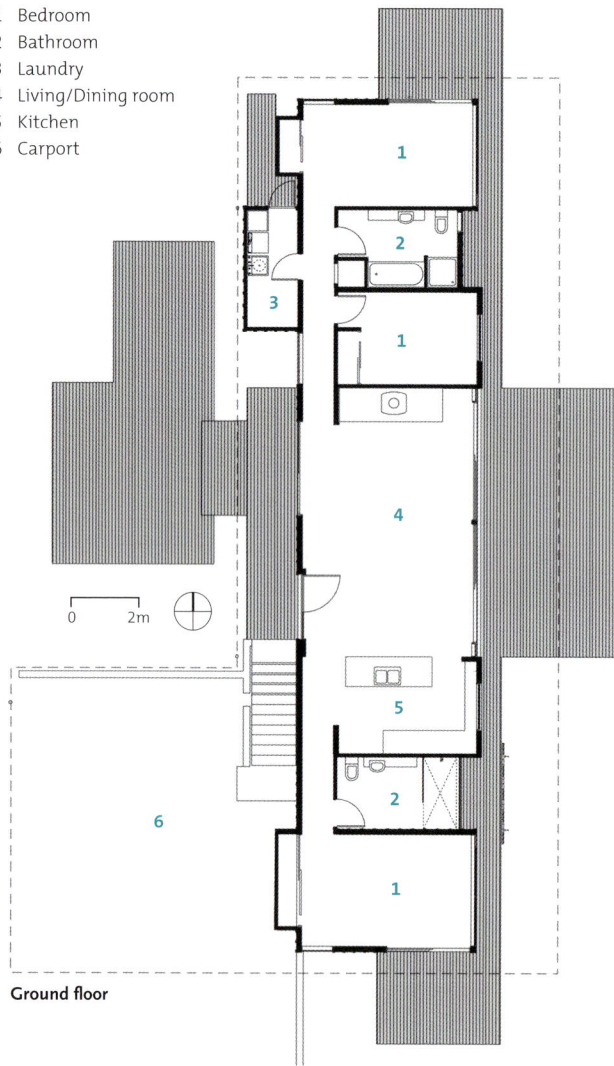

1 Bedroom
2 Bathroom
3 Laundry
4 Living/Dining room
5 Kitchen
6 Carport

0   2m

Ground floor

Barrow House

Brunswick, Victoria, Australia

Andrew Maynard Architects

Photography: Peter Bennetts

The Barrow extension appears as an arrangement of timber boxes, each independently rotated and subjected to varying amounts of extruding and manipulating forces. These separate actions result in a variety of shapes which, united, create an interior of differing volumes and organisations, providing an interesting double-storey addition to this weatherboard house.

The extension challenges the traditional nature of timber construction. Normally lightweight and fragile, added wall thickness to different areas results in a structure with a fluctuating sense of mass. The dynamic and varying nature of these environments is further enhanced by differing window arrangements and framing techniques. Frequently the windows are set back within the frame of the wall, sometimes flush and occasionally extruding beyond the timber frame.

This unconventional approach to massing and window design subverts the conservative planar nature of a 'box'. The movement of the shadows created by these extruding or intruding elements is tracked on the external facade and internal environment, creating varying patterns and giving the extension an undefined geometry. The strategic placement of a separate living space at the western end of the site reflects the focus of the site internally, frames the large open area and increases privacy levels.

The entirety of the design employs materials reused from the parts of the previous house as well as recycled or found elements, decreasing the carbon footprint of the design and also adding character to the spaces.

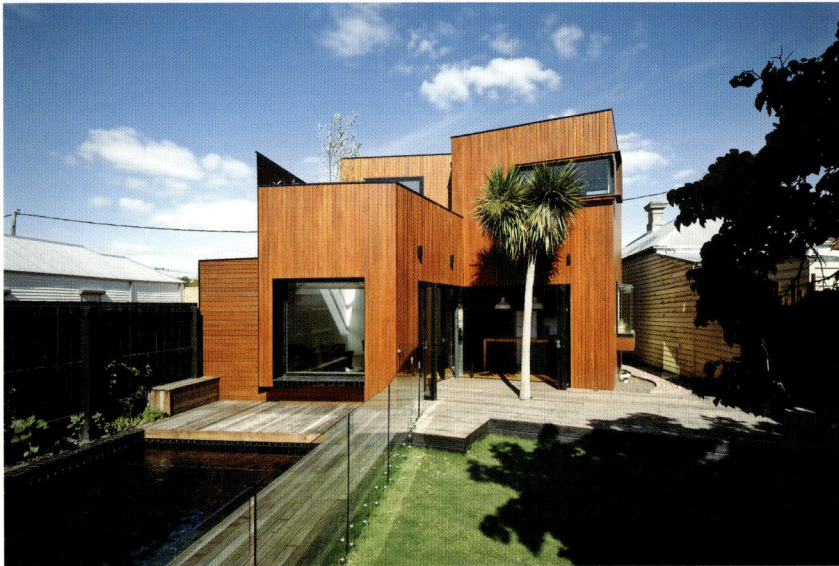

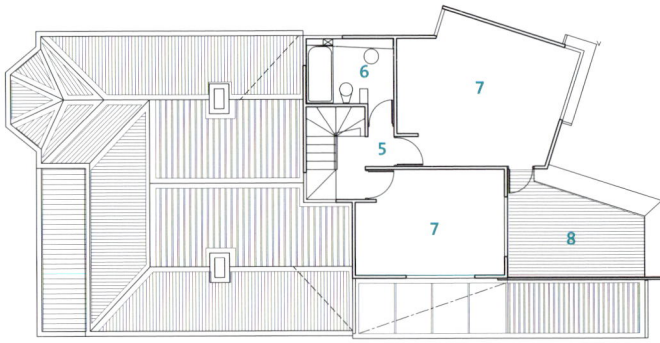

First floor

1 Living room
2 Dining room
3 Kitchen
4 Laundry/Pantry
5 Landing
6 Bathroom
7 Bedroom
8 Terrace
9 Pool
10 Studio
11 Garage

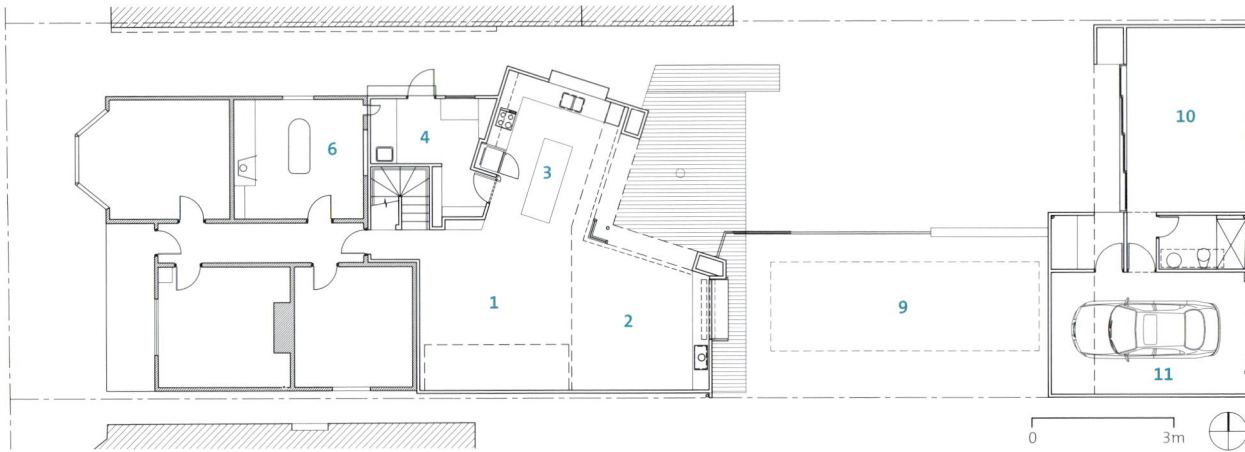

Ground floor

0   3m

Bayview House

Bronte, NSW, Australia

Kevin Ng, Brian Meyerson Architects

Photography: Brett Boardman

Bayview House is a new residence in Bronte, located on the sloping northern flank of the Bronte gully. The site has views over the adjacent park towards the beach and the ocean baths. The idea for the house was generated by inverting the typical planning arrangement—the living areas have been located on the upper floor, with the bedrooms on the lower floor. The living spaces thus capture the view and the natural light while the sleeping spaces benefit from the additional privacy at the ground level.

The architectural idea was realised by splitting the house into two distinct parts—upper and lower. The upper part is a suspended form with a strong C-shaped enclosing edge which serves to orientate the structure towards the view. In contrast, the lower part is a dark volume which recedes from view, serving to accentuate the floating nature of the form above. In order to refine the design, three types of glass were used—low-E, grey tint and colourback—implemented to insulate, provide privacy and conceal the structure respectively.

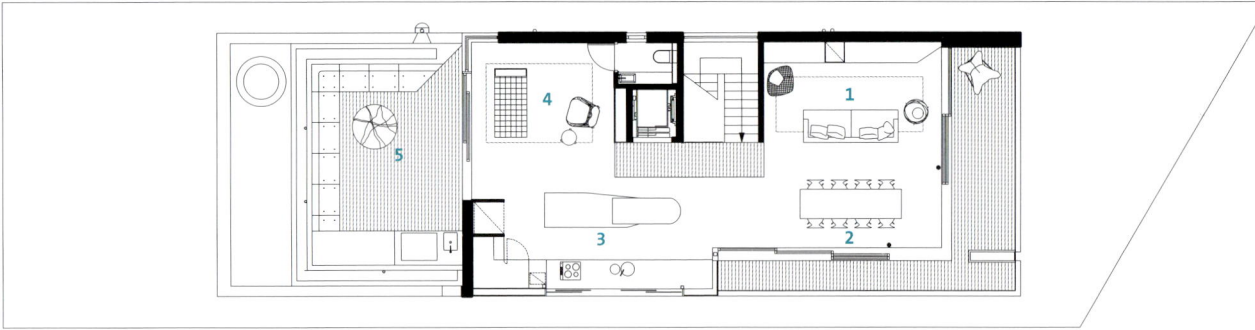

First floor

1 Living room
2 Dining room
3 Kitchen
4 Sitting room
5 Terrace

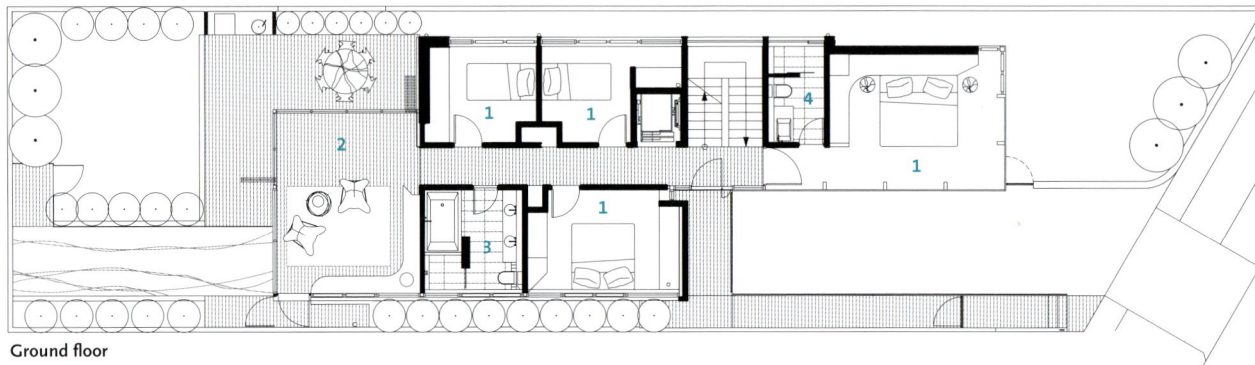

Ground floor

1 Bedroom
2 Rumpus room
3 Bathroom
4 Ensuite

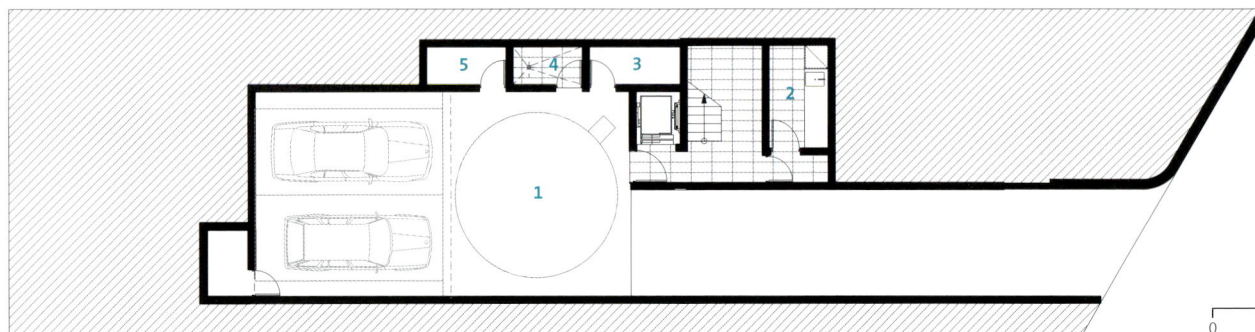

Basement

1 Garage
2 Laundry
3 Electrical
4 Garbage
5 Store room

0   4m

Beach House @ Point Lonsdale

Point Lonsdale, Victoria, Australia

Studio 101 Architects

Photography: Trevor Mein

This permanent beachside home, designed for a young family, is located in an established, heavily-treed native coastal environment. The rectilinear nature of the site and natural typography encouraged a simple yet highly efficient floor plan incorporating three pavilions linked by a continuous circulation spine. The eastern pavilion houses the sleeping and bathing zones, while the living zones are orientated to the north. Each pavilion is wrapped in a skin of white cypress that visually folds and interlocks with the expressed concrete block-work blade walls.

The primary living space, containing the kitchen, dining and living areas, floats above a masonry podium, cranking towards true north to maximise sun exposure and frame the elevated treed outlook. The primary block-work spine provides a continuity of materials from outside to within, allowing an honest and space-defining structural element that also provides for thermal mass to the internal environment.

Cross-flow ventilation is maximised through a combination of operable systems including sliding glazed doors and louvre windows, along with windows at both high and low levels. The central courtyard allows the house to breathe, and provides varying degrees of openness and intimacy, light and fresh air.

Sustainable living solutions include double-glazed windows with argon gas, rainwater harvested into a water tank, grey water reused for irrigation, while sustainably-managed timber and low-VOC coatings are used extensively. The result is a home that harmonises and integrates peacefully within its natural context.

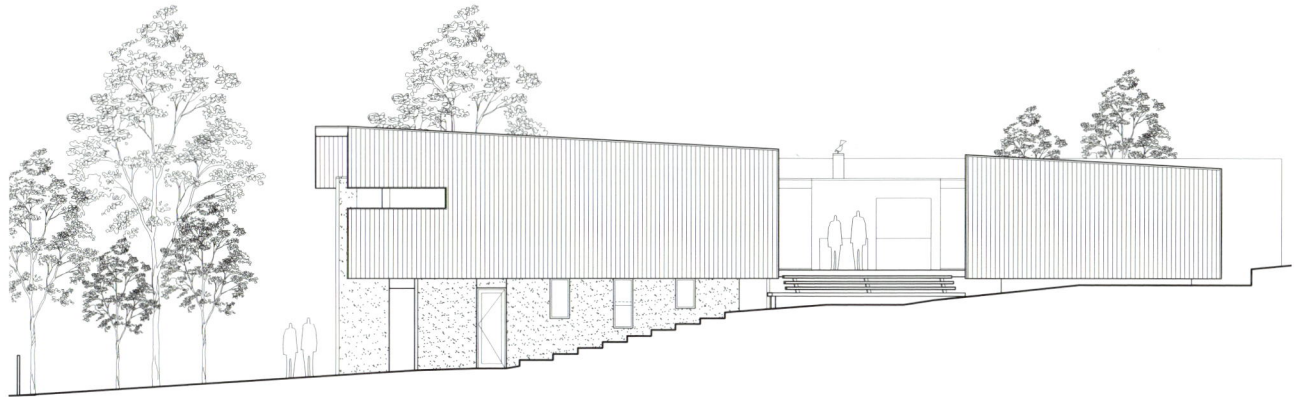

Elevation

1   Bedroom
2   Family room
3   Bathroom
4   Courtyard deck
5   Kitchen
6   Dining area
7   Living area
8   Powder room
9   Laundry
10 Ensuite
11 Garage
12 House undercroft
13 Entry
14 Entry deck
15 Studio

Ground floor

0   5m

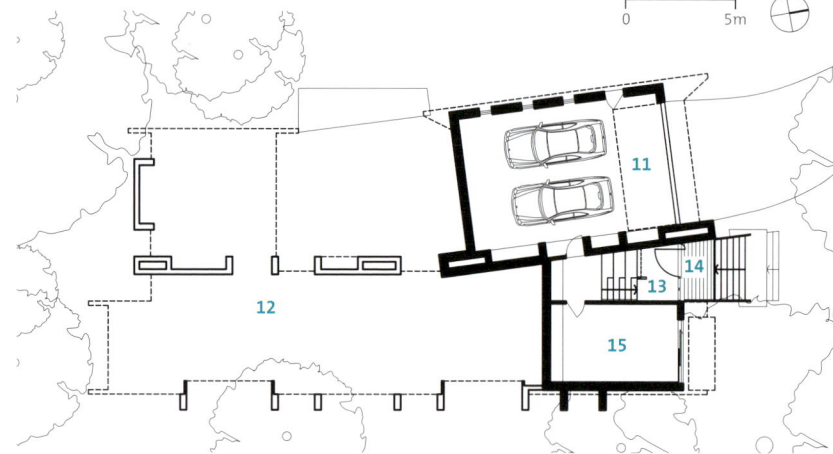

Lower ground floor

Beach Odyssey

Couran Point, South Stradbroke, Queensland, Australia

Kevin Hayes Architects

Photography: Scott Burrows and Matthew Jensen

Designed to accommodate up to 16 people, Beach Odyssey is a unique interpretation of the traditional Queensland beach house.

The rich timber exoskeleton wraps around and is wrapped around by the modern metallic Colorbond sheeting, creating a dramatic play on shadows that trace the passing of the day. The edges of the house are not definitive, but reach out into the land to merge with the landscape.

Circulation has been designed around an oversized main corridor, expressed through a series of columns and a double-height ceiling, which connects all the spaces. The bedsit, located over the garage, allows for the house to be used by two separate groups of holidaymakers, or can be used as a couple's retreat or a teenage hangout. The multiple decks located around the house also act as retreats, with private external day beds off all bedrooms, and the larger loft deck over the main deck.

Relationships between building elements have been played with in the design. Roofs turn down into walls, columns become walls, corners are exploded, roofs project and recess, walls fold into decks and floors, and the landscaping is folded into crevices and projections. This 'folding' element of the house adds a sense of movement and excitement, leading the eye across the facades and through to the waterways and landscape.

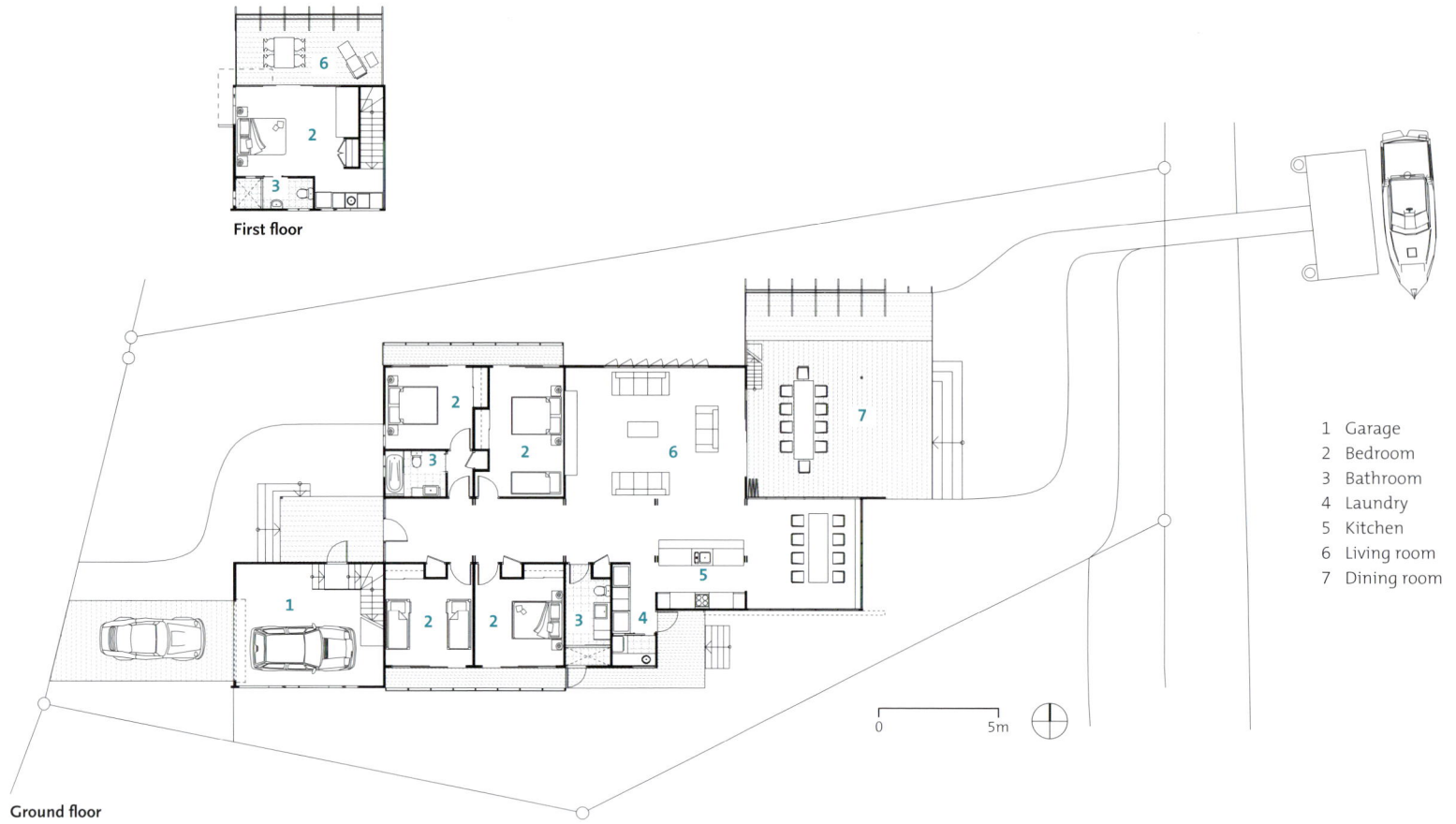

First floor

Ground floor

1 Garage
2 Bedroom
3 Bathroom
4 Laundry
5 Kitchen
6 Living room
7 Dining room

0   5m

Beached House

Coastal Victoria, Australia

BKK Architects

Photography: Peter Bennetts

Beached House continues BKK Architects' interest in the curation of the domestic as a sequence of unfolding spaces that deny, and then release, views. The journey throughout the house is undertaken via a series of subtly shifting spaces that alter one's orientation to climate and terrain.

Beached House has been conceived formally as an exercise in volumetric origami—the folding of spaces over and upon each other. In this way, the house resembles a small village or informal site occupation that has aggregated over time. There are a number of these folded spatial sequences within the house that allow for playful discovery and encounter as well as opportunities for varying connections between spaces.

The home offers the owners various readings and differing options for occupation. It is intended that living in the house will be an unfolding series of moments, linked closely to climate and site, that will continually delight and surprise.

1	Bedroom	8	Kitchen
2	Ensuite	9	Pool
3	Deck	10	Powder room
4	Retreat	11	Laundry/Wet room
5	Hall	12	Store room
6	Lounge	13	Entry
7	Dining room	14	Walk-in robe

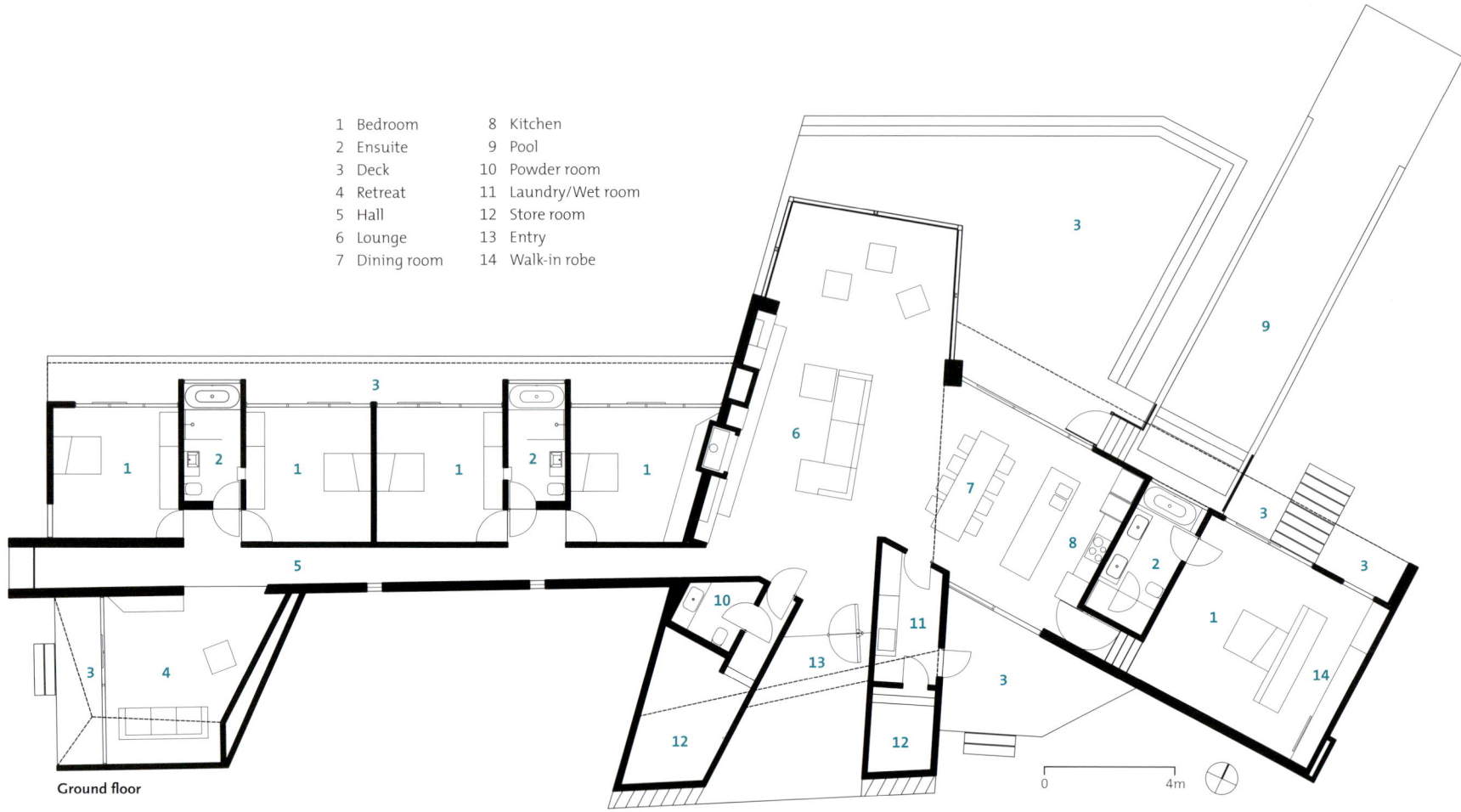

Ground floor

54

Boolarong and Kinkabool

Point Lookout, Queensland, Australia

BVN Architecture

Photography: Shane Thompson/
Christopher Frederick Jones

This is a modest development for two small detached houses on an elevated 817-square-metre site. The two houses are generally identical, with differences only occurring in response to the particular site location. The design is influenced by the need to comply with the requirements of the town plan and with a contemporary interpretation of an architectural form and character derived from aspects of the earlier houses developed in the older part of Point Lookout, on North Stradbroke Island.

The houses are arranged over three levels: the lower level providing car accommodation in an open carport arrangement along with an entry, open stair, laundry space and storage areas; the mid level, with three bedrooms and two small bathrooms; and the upper level, with a kitchen bench to one side of a single large living/dining area opening out to the generous lanai/veranda, a large covered outdoor living area designed to take advantage of the available views.

The elevations of the house incorporating the elevated upper levels over a generally open lower level, with flush matte terracotta tiles and openable timber stained batten screens, have been simply and carefully composed for an understated contemporary architectural form which also draws on the vernacular of the old Point Lookout.

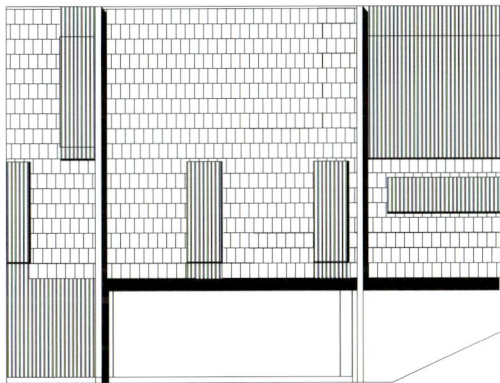

East elevation

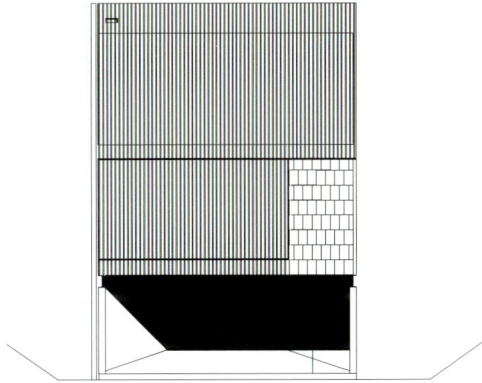

North elevation

Ground floor

First floor

Second floor

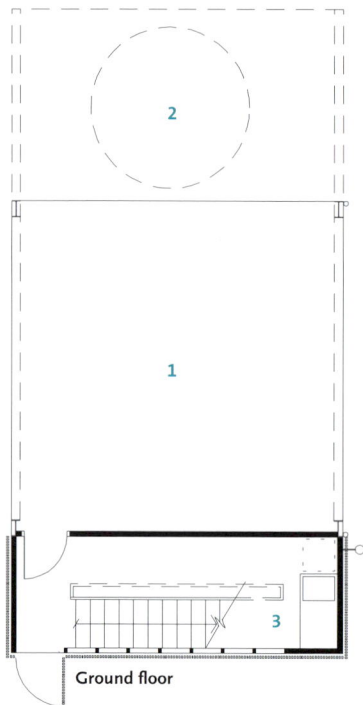

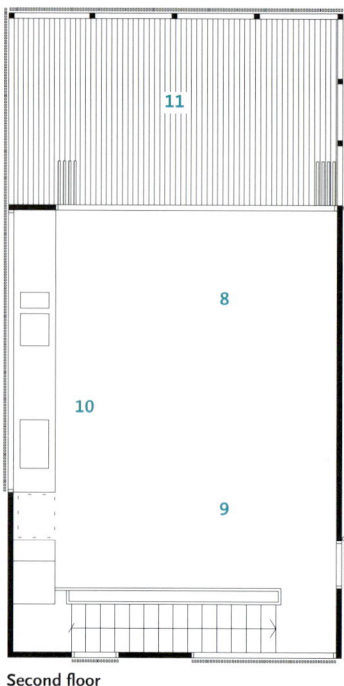

1 Garage
2 Underground water tank
3 Laundry
4 Master bedroom
5 Bedroom
6 Multi-purpose room
7 Bathroom
8 Living room
9 Dining room
10 Kitchen
11 Lanai

0   2m

Brighton House

Brighton East, Victoria, Australia

Edwin Halim and Michael McKenna

Photography: Trevor Mein

This single family house, located on a corner allotment in Brighton, replaces a suburban brick villa. The design is a response to planning controls for open space, building envelopes, heights and setbacks. It maintains established gardens and mature trees, yet fulfils the client brief for a unique family home.

The dual-level design stratifies function zones with ground-floor garage and living areas, and upper-floor bedrooms areas. The dual levels are interconnected by two voids, providing a seamless transition of space through the interior. The ground-floor main living room is open plan, integrating kitchen and dining.

The architecture has a classic modernist profile emphasising white cubic elements, oversailing roof and suspended balcony in a composite of wood, metal and render.

The interior has a serene off-white painted plaster with timber flooring that provides a neutral ambience to accentuate the client's collection of Javanese timber fitments and furniture.

Timber is used extensively for both structure and finish, and was a key strategy for delivering the house on budget where crafted carpenter's detailing prevails.

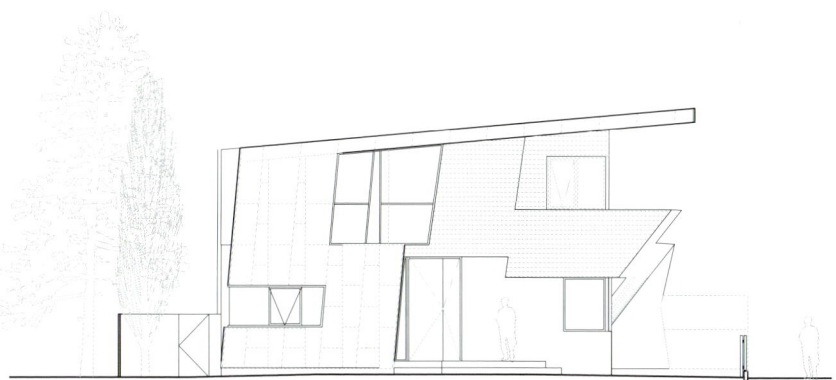

South elevation

Ground floor

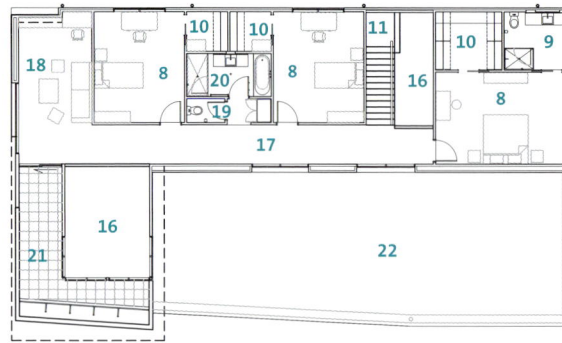

First floor

1 Entry
2 Living room
3 Dining room
4 Kitchen
5 Study
6 Powder room
7 Store room
8 Bedroom
9 Ensuite
10 Robe
11 Stair

12 Family room
13 Terrace
14 Laundry
15 Garage
16 Void
17 Gallery
18 Family room
19 WC
20 Bathroom
21 Balcony
22 Roof below

0 3m

Bulimba Boathouse

Bulimba, Queensland, Australia

Owen and Vokes

Photography: Jon Linkins

The site of the Bulimba Boathouse is a small, 10-metre-wide lot. Naturally enough, a small lot calls for a small house.

Scale is a matter of perception. The approach taken to scale on this project was to manipulate one's perception of both the scale of the house and the scale of its setting. A singular open-plan diagram was discarded in favour of numerous smaller rooms, each with their defining character, offering a generous suite of spatial experiences, multiple orientations, and varied relationships with the settings.

Due to the initiatives of urban consolidation, public and private open space is being lost to more buildings. The character of Brisbane Town, and its historic low-density setting, is under threat. The philosophy behind Bulimba Boathouse is based on the premise that humans are biologically predisposed to liking natural settings. A close proximity to nature—a view of trees, blue sky or the stars—increases the chances for contentment. Accordingly, preferred room types, the peninsula and the walled garden are deployed in an attempt to idealise the presence of nature in the setting. This particular planning approach values gardens over car accommodation and extra rooms, and enables a genuine contribution to the private open space of the city.

First floor

1 Bedroom
2 Walk-in-robe
3 Study
4 Ensuite
5 Bathroom

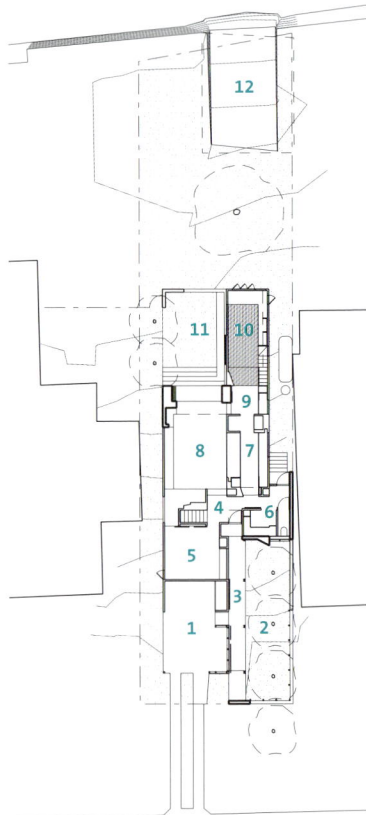

1 Carport
2 Street garden
3 Loggia
4 Vestibule
5 Sitting room
6 Laundry
7 Kitchen
8 Family room
9 Office
10 Library
11 River garden
12 Boat shed

0   5m

Ground floor

Butterley House

Wanniassa, ACT, Australia

Nathan Gibson Judd Architecture

Photography: Brett Boardman

Butterley House is a modest detached house on a small site, behind an existing dwelling on a corner block. The house resonates with its 1970s suburban context through the use of dry-pressed Simmental silver bricks, skillion roofs, raked ceilings, internal masonry, aluminium windows, concrete floors, external decks, and a roof terrace.

The sequential spaces—starting with the kitchen, dining room, courtyard and living room—establish a sense of progression and depth, with a mature apple tree acting as the ultimate focal point.

The ground-floor living spaces flow indoor to outdoor, creating a strong relationship with the external environment. Established trees have been maintained, forming a natural screen to the north and protecting the privacy of occupants. The house orients the living areas along the north side of an east–west single-skin brick spine, and the facade is generously punched with glazed openings that, together with an inset courtyard, produces rooms that are engaged with the garden.

The dining area, directly below the roof terrace, is backed by the brick spine wall that runs through the house, separating the living and service areas of the house.

The roof terrace and generous glazing to the ensuite and master bedroom frame views of the Brindabella mountain range.

1 Living room
2 Bedroom
3 Deck
4 Bathroom
5 Laundry
6 Kitchen/Dining room
7 Office
8 Courtyard
9 Roof terrace

0   7m

Ground floor

First floor

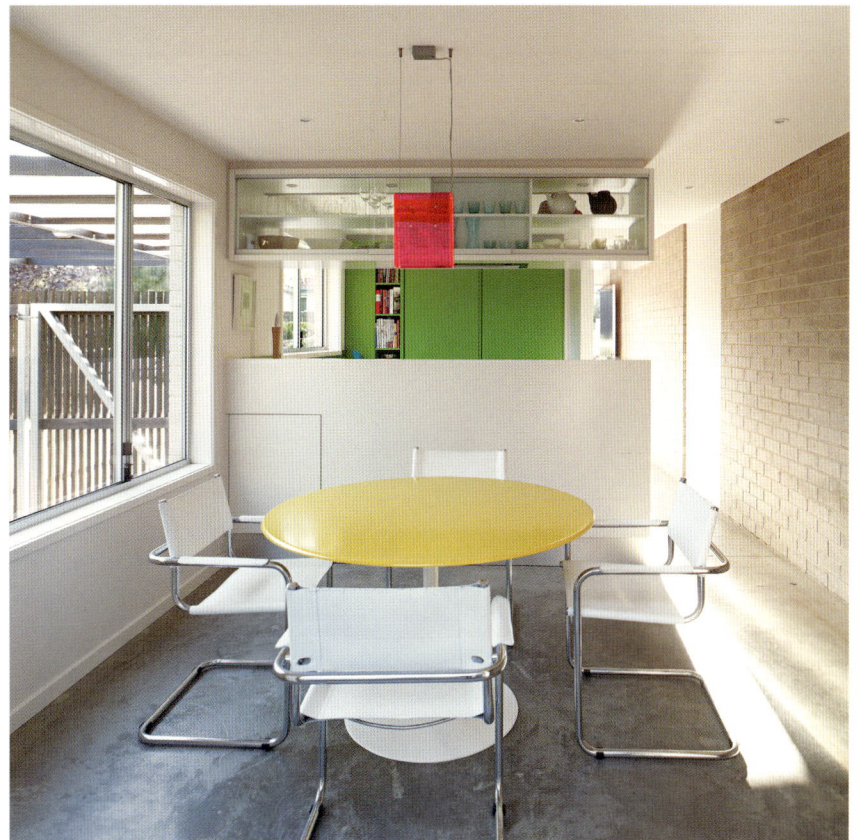

Carlton House

Carlton, Victoria, Australia

Nic Owen Architects

Photography: Rhiannon Slatter

This addition is located on a very small site at the rear of an existing Victorian terrace in lively Carlton. The solution was a modern addition which, while reading as visually separate to the existing building, does not overpower or compromise the integrity of the small worker's cottage.

The use of stacked concrete blocks for the addition links the new building to the cobblestones seen in the laneways wrapping around the site and bluestone base of the existing cottage. The materials palette has been limited to the use of concrete, a ribbon of form-ply which grounds the house while discretely hiding the garage door, vertical spotted-gum timber cladding and black aluminium windows and doors.

Critical to the brief was the ability to accommodate more private living space, reducing noise in the existing building and incorporating a multipurpose room which doubles as a garage or a second living room in the future. In a further effort to use all available space, the roof area in the existing cottage was fitted out to create an artist's studio.

This three-bedroom residence on a small inner-city site offers an environmentally responsible solution to compact sustainable living.

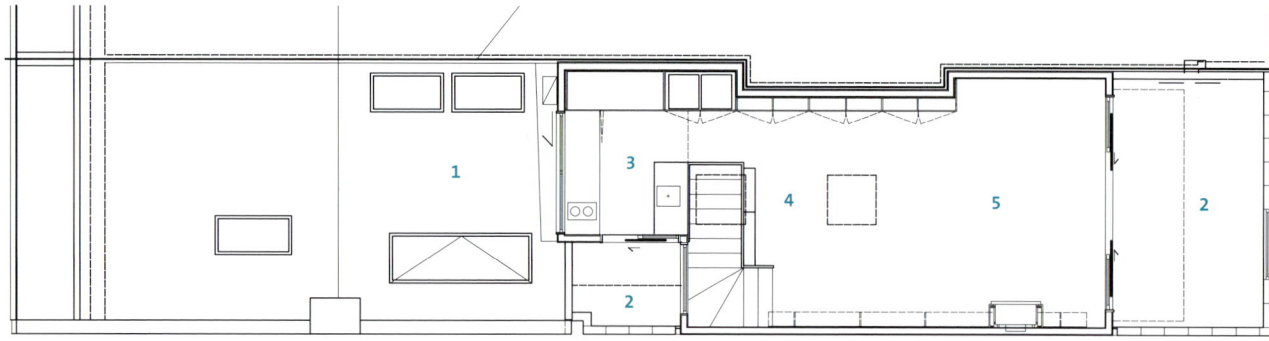

First floor

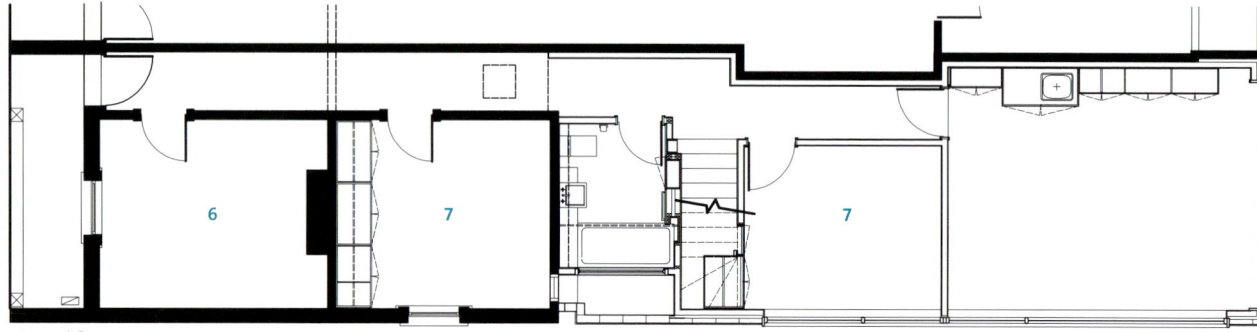

Ground floor

1 Studio   5 Family room
2 Balcony   6 Office
3 Kitchen   7 Bedroom
4 Meals area

0   3m

The Caulfield House

Caulfield, Victoria, Australia

Bower Architecture

Photography: Shannon McGrath

The brief was to design a bold and efficient new house with the flexibility to accommodate varying numbers of family, visitors and guests. The resulting house strives for a balance between street presence and harmony with its surrounding buildings, engaging passers-by through its sculptural form and teasing glimpses which invite curiosity, while preserving privacy within.

Externally, zinc and concrete conceal a peaceful interior retreat, bathed in natural light. Varied north-facing living volumes across both floor levels, ranging in scale from expansive to intimate, are arranged around, behind and above a central courtyard. The courtyard is joined to each volume in a different way, transforming a corridor into an outdoor reading room or adding to the volume of living areas. Natural light, winter sun and passive cross-ventilation are brought into and through these areas by a central gallery and louvred clerestory, which run along the central spine of the house.

The house continually balances and reveals itself along the journey through its spaces, using the play of natural light, openness, variation in volume, clarity of form and use of sustainable, refined and raw materials—aspects essential in contemporary architecture.

1 Entry
2 Garage
3 Study
4 Laundry
5 Bedroom
6 Gallery
7 Living room
8 Courtyard
9 Reading alcove
10 Service kitchen
11 Kitchen and meals
12 Family room
13 Deck
14 Pond
15 Water feature
16 BBQ
17 Void
18 Rumpus room

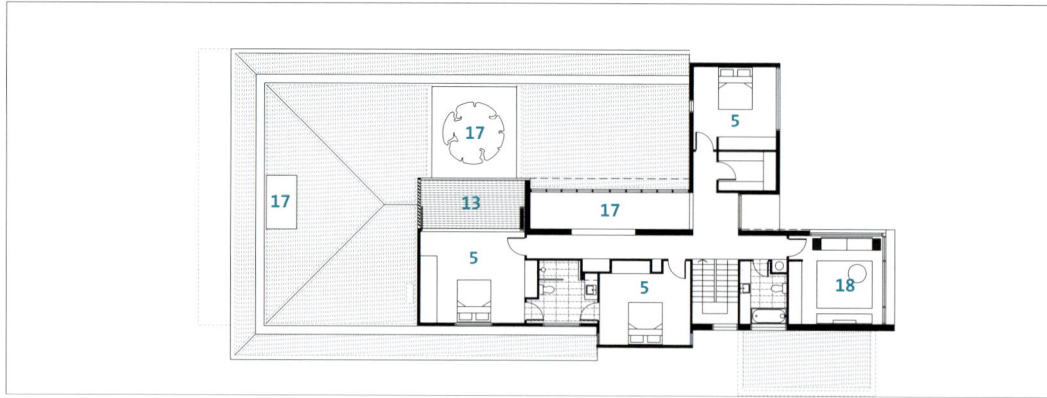

First floor

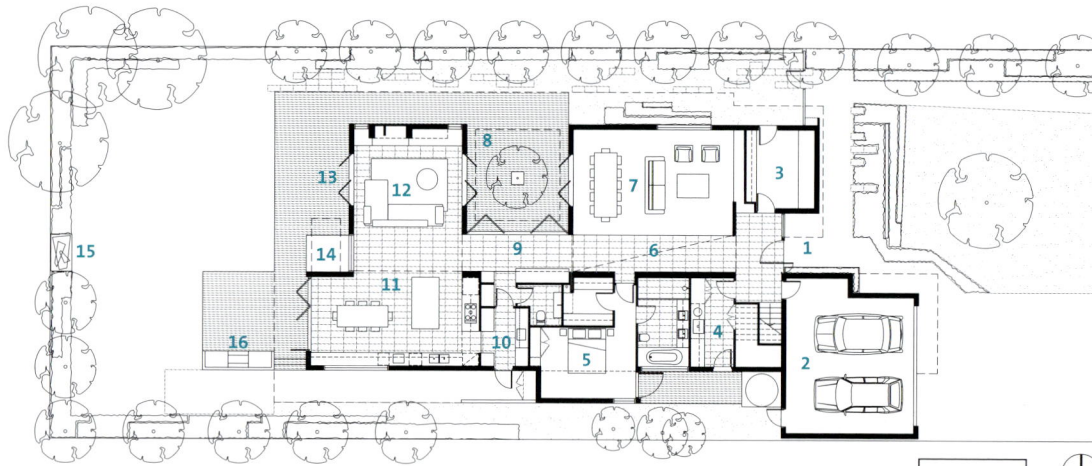

Ground floor

0   5m

Cliffbrook House

Clovelly, NSW, Australia

To1 Architecture & Interiors

Photography: Brett Boardman

Cliffbrook House was an alterations and additions to a dilapidated and dysfunctional house that sat on a superb cliff-top site overlooking Gordons Bay, immediately south of Clovelly.

After acquiring the site, the client engaged the architects to redesign the house to better capitalise on its position. As it was also to be a functional family home, the residence needed to be more than just a viewing platform.

The initial client design brief referenced the concrete bunker, a defensive military fortification that would sit comfortably camouflaged within the cliff-face and surrounding environment. The project became an experiment in form and materiality, embracing the overt beauty of the location, the spectacular views out over the Pacific, and the site's other, more subtle charms—the smell of the salt, and the colours and texture of the sandstone cliffs.

The raw concrete entry, intended to evoke the unpolished, eroded nature of the site, is on the middle level and leads into a large open plan living/dining/kitchen area that serves as the family's primary space. Below, in the lower level, are the children's bedrooms and a media room. The upper storey houses a master suite that looks to the south-west, out over the Pacific.

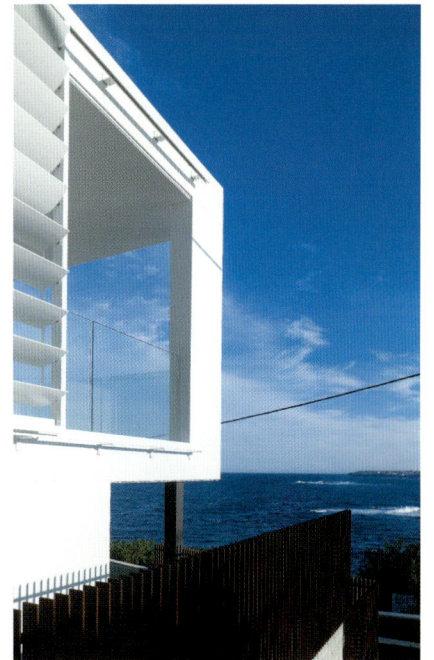

1 Storage
2 Bedroom
3 Bathroom
4 WC
5 Living room
6 Media room
7 Garage
8 Laundry
9 Terrace
10 Dining room
11 Entry
12 Kitchen
13 Courtyard
14 Walk-in-robe
15 Ensuite
16 Master bedroom
17 Study

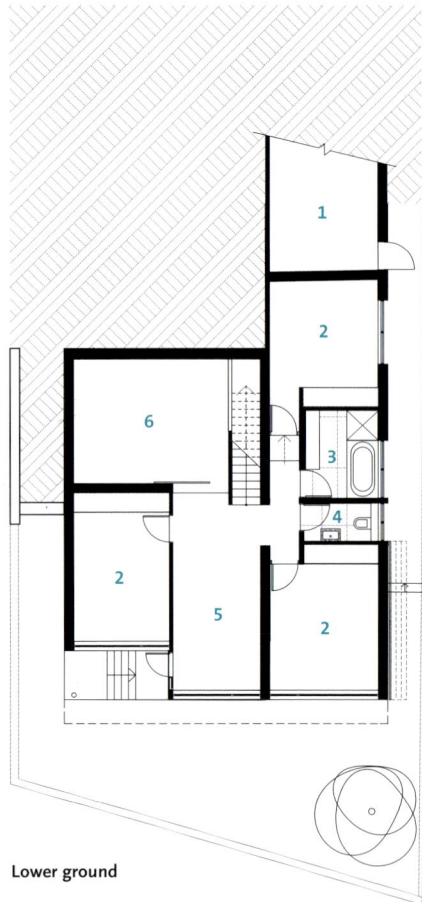

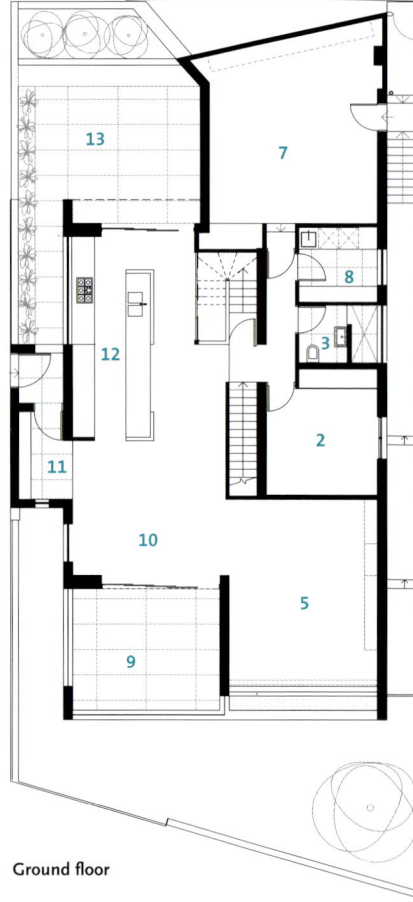

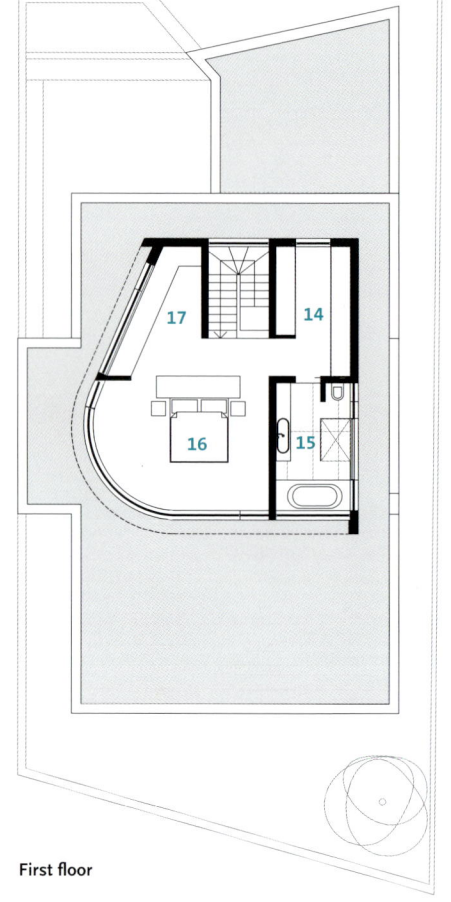

0   4m

Lower ground

Ground floor

First floor

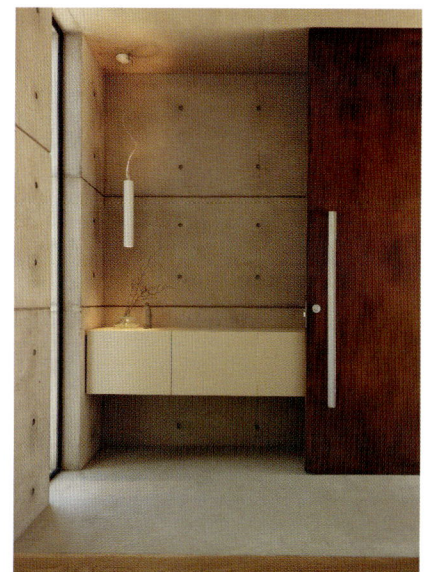

Clifton Hill House

Clifton Hill, Victoria, Australia

Nic Owen Architects

Photography: Rhiannon Slatter

This project aimed to restore the original Victorian cottage while creating a contemporary and exciting piece of architecture at the rear. Paying respect to the original form was of utmost importance, as was designing and building a new space that was well and truly in the 21st century. Marrying the two in a sympathetic and respectful manner created both the challenge and excitement of this project.

The brief included a three/four bedroom, two-bathroom house with a study. The living area consists of an open-plan kitchen/dining room/lounge delineated by the use of plywood bulkheads. The successful collaboration between the client, architect and builder has resulted in a project that is a source of pleasure for the client and pride for both the builder and architect. The passionate vision and drive maintained throughout the project has seen the successful marrying of artistic design with function, satisfying the client's brief and the architect's creative dreams.

First floor

1 Bathroom
2 Bedroom
3 Canopy

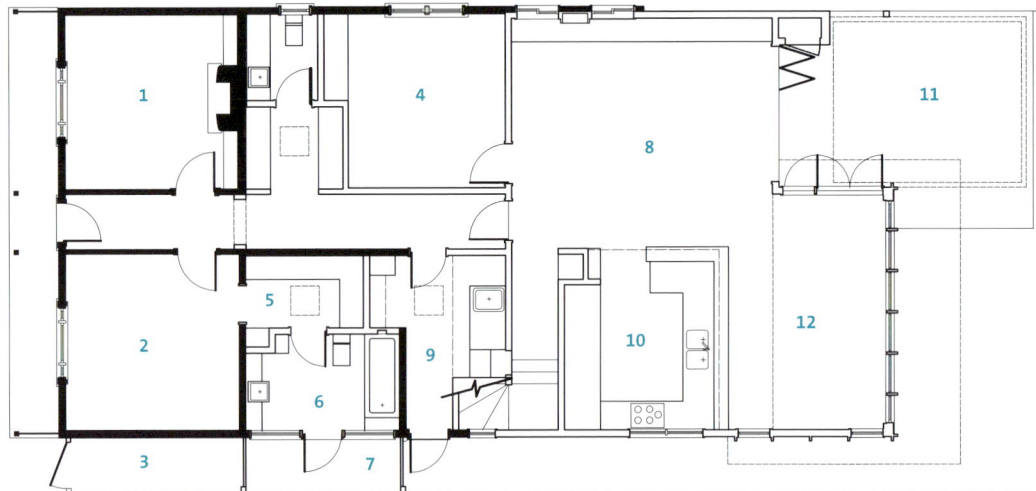

0   3m

Ground floor

1 Study
2 Bedroom
3 Store room
4 Rumpus room
5 Walk-in-robe
6 Ensuite
7 Courtyard
8 Family room
9 Laundry
10 Kitchen
11 Deck
12 Meals area

Elysium 154

Noosaville, Queensland, Australia

BVN Architecture

Photography: Christopher Frederick Jones

The site for this project demanded respect and sensitivity to take maximum advantage of its seclusion and natural beauty while also acknowledging the close proximity of neighbouring properties. The preferred design approach was to respond to the landscape character and climate of the area and to emphasise outdoor, or almost outdoor, living.

The house enjoys a wide variety of living spaces, from the more hermetic retreat of the media room at ground level to the two-storey-high spaces of the more formal living/dining area, which flows smoothly out onto a large outdoor pool terrace. The north-western corner is dedicated to larger but more informal spaces for the kitchen and family areas, including a large bay window. An upper level includes bedrooms and a study, with a large master bedroom overlooking the northern garden and adjoining parkland.

The sweeping curved walls and forms, which identify the house, are generated by a partly intuitive and partly analytical response to achieve both a north-east aspect and views to the northern parklands areas. The soft curves of the three major walls that define the house also offer a dynamic feeling to both the interior spaces and external form.

Elysium 154 offers a relaxed mode of contemporary sub-tropical living with a quality of experience, finish, materials and character that, while drawing on the modernist tradition, is particular to the house's site and a further development of the regional resort typology.

1 Garage
2 Store room
3 Terrace
4 Pool
5 Media room
6 Powder room
7 Laundry
8 Kitchen
9 Day bed
10 Family room
11 Dining/Living room
12 Bedroom
13 Balcony
14 Bathroom
15 Study

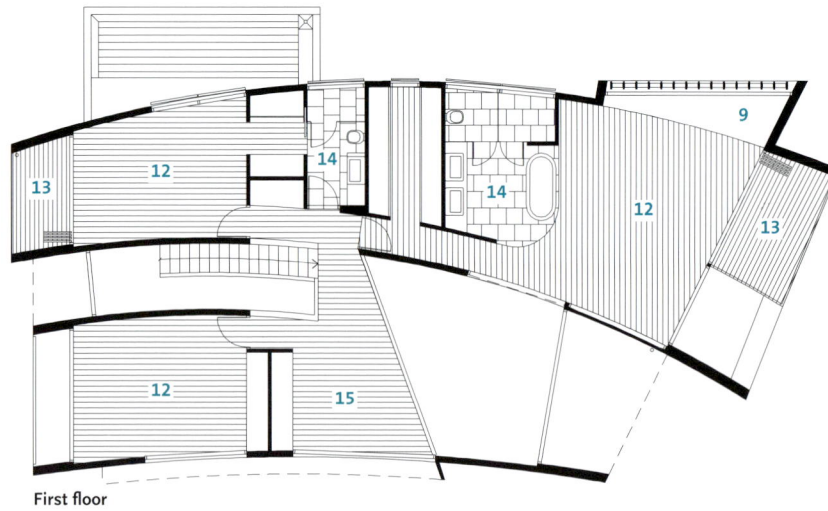

First floor

Ground floor

0   6m

90

Elysium 169

Noosaville, Queensland, Australia

BVN Architecture

Photography: Christopher Frederick Jones

The provision of adequate privacy, sun protection from the north and west, and deeply shaded outdoor living areas informed the principal formal gesture of a large single-storey screen to the upper level of the house, which generally floats above the more deeply recessed lower levels, incorporating large areas of retractable glazing which afford ambiguous separation between interior and exterior. This screen is then manipulated through cuts, folds and penetrations in response to the upper-level uses and lower-level demands for sun shading. Further flexibility for privacy and comfort is facilitated by finely detailed timer screening systems.

The house has no distinctive 'front', and could be perceived as being more a pavilion given the elevation and prominence of its location.

Accordingly, this exposure and prominence has affected the larger composition of external landscape, screen walls and house proper as a holistic composition.

The planning ensures that the principal living areas and master bedroom suite take maximum advantage of the views and aspect, while secondary bedrooms and service areas are located to the south and east. A central internal stair provides easy but discreet access to the upper-level bedrooms, and the two-storey-high living/dining areas further facilitate efficient cross-ventilation to all spaces. The construction and materials employed are traditional and prosaic but manipulated in a more refined and considered manner than might normally be expected.

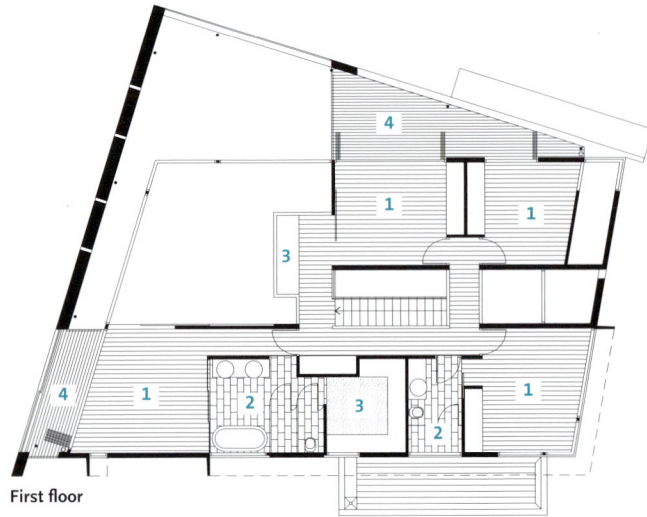

First floor

1 Bedroom
2 Bathroom
3 Walk-in-robe
4 Deck

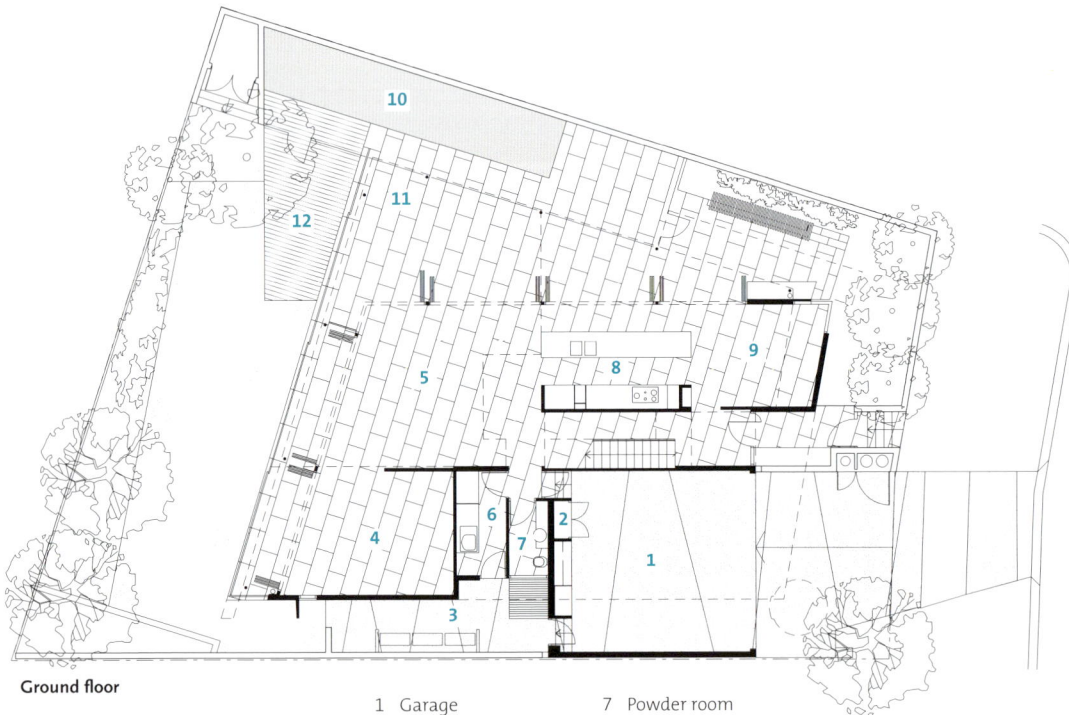

Ground floor

1	Garage	7	Powder room
2	Store	8	Kitchen
3	Service/Drying court	9	Family room
4	Media room	10	Pool
5	Living/Dining room	11	Terrace
6	Laundry	12	Deck

0   4m

Fig Tree Pocket River House

Brisbane, Queensland, Australia

Bligh Graham Architects

Photography: Jon Linkins

This dramatic, steep site overlooking the Brisbane River presented a major challenge, with the views and slope to the south making access to northern light and winter sun difficult. The C-shaped courtyard plan resolved this by providing all the principal rooms, including those overlooking the river, with a northern aspect. The courtyard also enables summer breezes to penetrate the house, while creating an intimate garden sheltered from the strong winter 'westerlies' and the summer storms coming up the river. This courtyard space is hidden from view, revealed only upon entry into the house proper.

In contrast to this captured landscape, the outdoor room at the end of the entry axis launches out 6 metres above the ground, enabling breathtaking views up and down the river. In the courtyard, the ground plane is reconfigured to yield both an upper garden that relates to the living level and a lower pond that is overlooked by the main bedroom suite. The drama of these spaces is amplified by the flanking pool, which projects out towards the river. The crisp, tropical modernism of the house exterior is played off against the warmth of the timber-lined courtyard and interior spaces, creating a timeless family home.

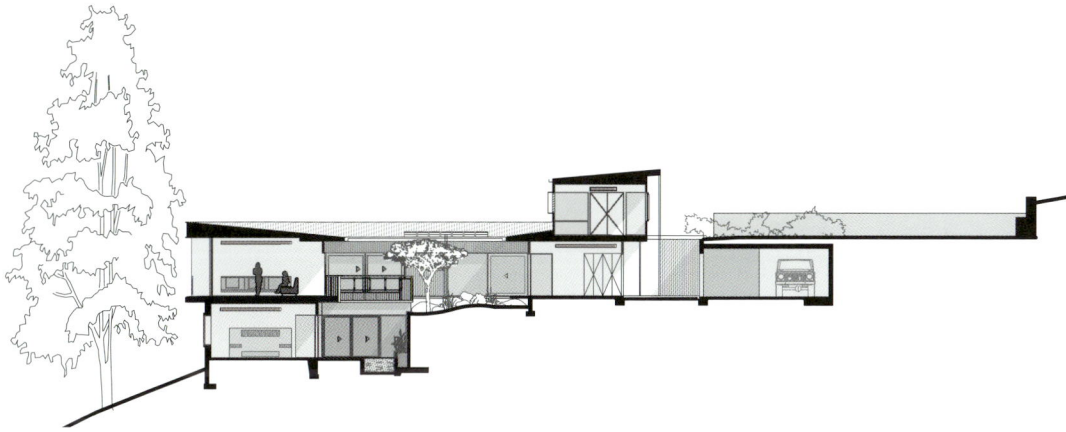
Section

First floor

1 Bathroom
2 Bedroom
3 Lawn

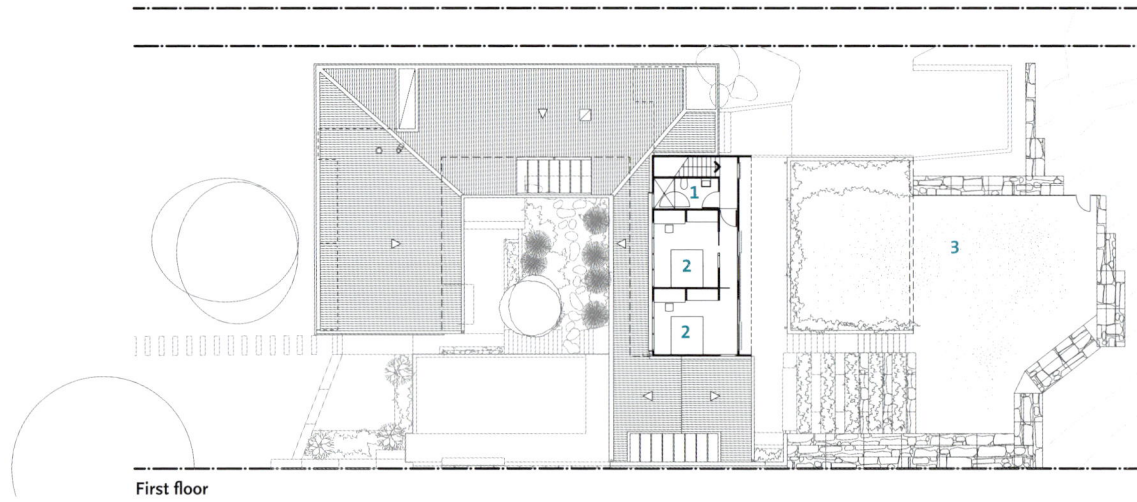

Ground floor

1 Outdoor room
2 Living/Dining area
3 Kitchen
4 Pantry
5 Study
6 Entry deck
7 Laundry
8 Powder room
9 Dog kennel
10 Rumpus room
11 Garage
12 Store room
13 Change room
14 Driveway
15 Deck
16 Drying court
17 Pool terrace
18 Pool
19 Courtyard

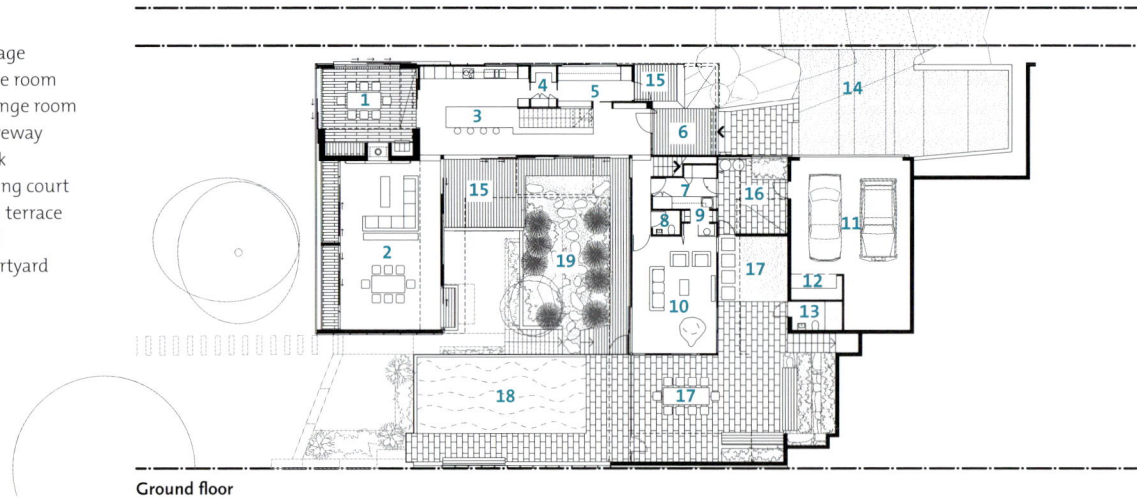

Lower ground floor

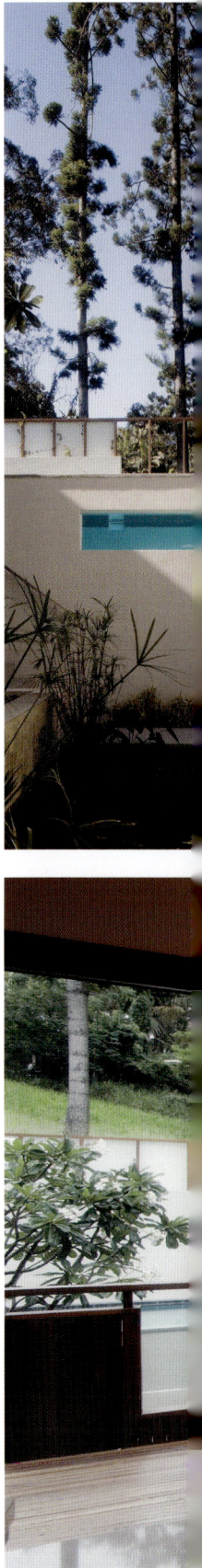

1 Bedroom
2 Exercise room
3 Plant room
4 Bathroom
5 Ensuite
6 Walk-in-robe
7 Main bedroom
8 Sunken court with lily pond

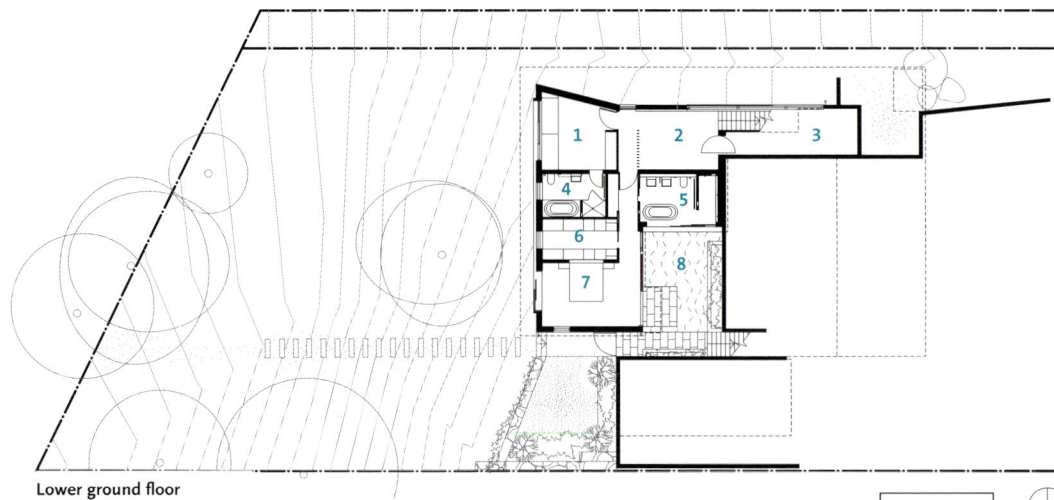

0   6m

Fitzroy North House

Fitzroy North, Victoria, Australia

Nic Owen Architects

Photography: Rhiannon Slatter

This renovation is located on a small site in North Fitzroy with tight planning and heritage controls and a challenging orientation. The owners of the small Victorian terrace approached the architects with a brief to create a larger house with a bright and airy feel to cater for their growing family.

A modern glass structure wrapped in a timber skin formed the shell of the extension, providing light and vertical space while maintaining the south neighbour's access to light. New works are recessive and respectful, and complement the historic setting. Full-height windows with fixed metal blades on the north laneway provide privacy from within and allow winter sunlight to enter through an open glass and timber stairwell. Large skylights add to the sense of space and light. North-facing roofs accommodate photovoltaic cells and solar hot-water panels, and plantation timbers have been used throughout.

This three-bedroom inner-city residence on a small site offers a sympathetic response to historically sensitive inner-city living.

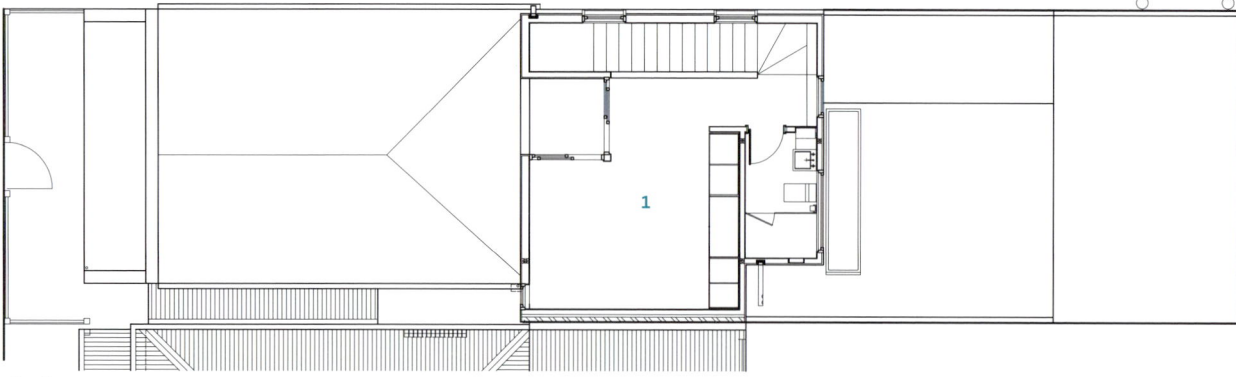

First floor

Ground floor

1 Bedroom
2 Living
3 Kitchen

0   2m

Fleurieu Beach House

Fleurieu, South Australia, Australia

Max Pritchard Architect

Photography: Sam Noonan

Sweeping views of hills, beach, rocks and ocean inspired the fan-shaped plan form of this two-level holiday house, with the clients wanting a relaxing holiday house that capitalised on the views to the north and east. The long, arcing plan form follows the shape of the land, built into the hillside, resulting in a form sympathetic to site levels, views and sun.

Corrugated iron and timber were used in the construction, being timeless materials and appropriate to a rural coastal context.

Large bifold doors open out onto generous timber decking, and the kitchen extends out to a sheltered barbeque area, encouraging a relaxed holiday lifestyle.

There is a sense of privacy and interest from the street, with the curved walls of timber and iron, but on entering, the full extent of the spectacular view is revealed through the sweeping arc of glass and the sculptural stair which, along with the strong colours and bright furniture, add to the sense of fun and relaxation.

Orientation for winter solar gain, durable economical materials, functional design and sculptural form makes Fleurieu Beach House a model for holiday houses in this unique bay.

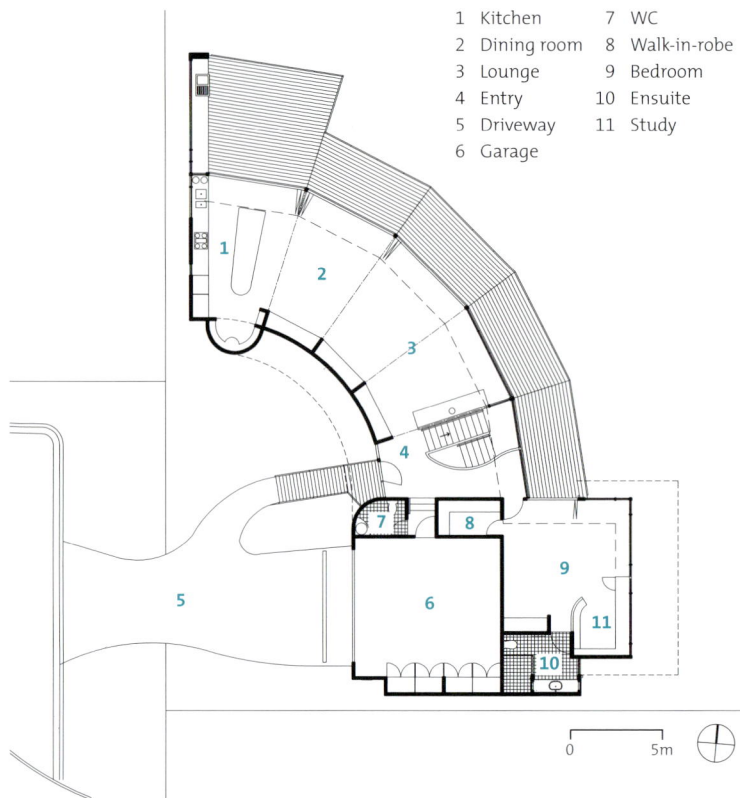

1	Kitchen	7	WC
2	Dining room	8	Walk-in-robe
3	Lounge	9	Bedroom
4	Entry	10	Ensuite
5	Driveway	11	Study
6	Garage		

0   5m

First floor

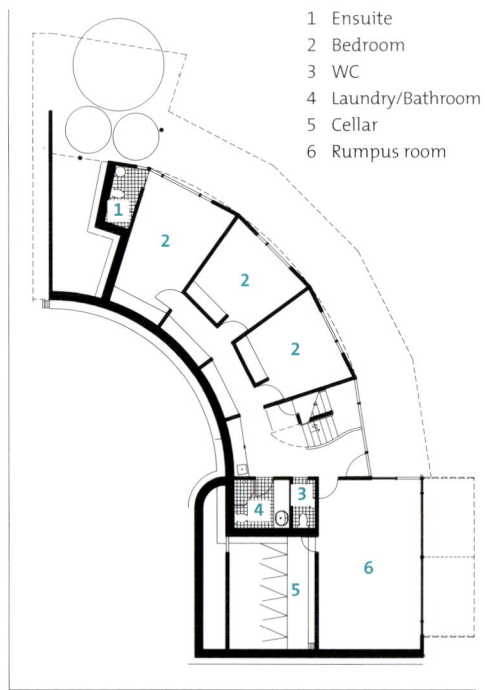

1 Ensuite
2 Bedroom
3 WC
4 Laundry/Bathroom
5 Cellar
6 Rumpus room

Ground floor

Gold Street House

Brunswick, Victoria, Australia

Kavellaris Urban Design

Photography: Peter Bennetts

The Gold Street House responds to the rear laneway-like character which consists of garage doors, timber backyard fences and at times neglected leftover spaces from the terrace houses that front the opposing street. These homes (like many terrace typologies) abandoned the rear of their terraces fronting Gold Street, and in doing so over the years cultivated a language of gable/hipped roof building forms and utilitarian lean-to structures constructed of lightweight material such as compressed sheet—a very low-tech, economically-driven decision.

The response was to celebrate and reinterpret the context rather than pretend it was not there. The strategy was to insert a galvanized-steel portal frame that encompasses the entire perimeter of the structure. The structural element is diagrammatically and symbolically translated as the 'symbol' of a 'house' as opposed to a simple ambiguous and anonymous out building.

The materiality of the house incorporates and engages with the architectural language surrounding the contextual vernacular of black-metal wall and roof cladding, painted compressed sheeting and timber panelling. By critically arranging these materials and their application, the house proudly and boldly addresses the street in its bright red and purple colours.

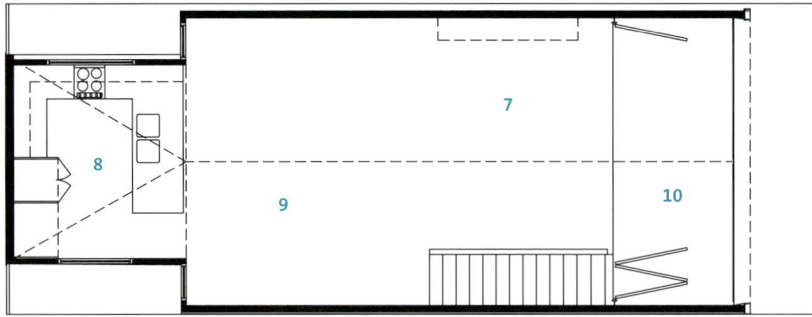

First floor

7 Living room
8 Kitchen
9 Dining room
10 Balcony

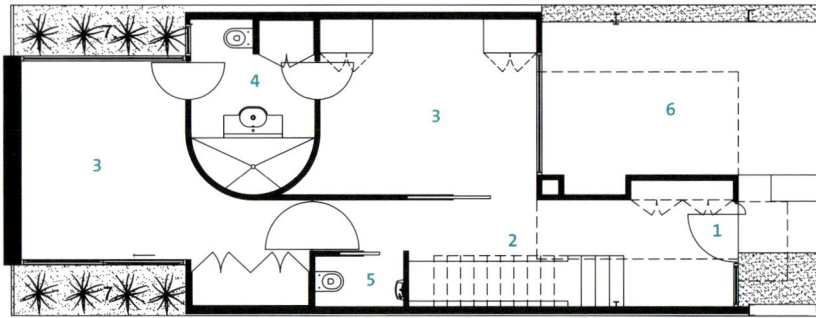

Ground floor

1 Entry foyer
2 Study
3 Bedroom
4 Ensuite
5 WC
6 Carport

1 Entry foyer   7   Living room
2 Study   8   Kitchen
3 Bedroom   9   Dining room
4 Ensuite   10 Balcony
5 WC   11 Laundry/Cellar
6 Carport

0   2m

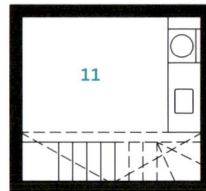

Lower floor

Gordonton House

Gordonton, North Island, New Zealand

Frans Kamermans

Photography: Architect and owner

Gordonton House is a contemporary interpretation of the traditional New Zealand rural weatherboard vernacular. Designed on a pattern of 'barn-form' pavilions, which separate the components of the plan, this house makes full use of the generous 6701-square-metre site area.

Traditionally detailed, the 378-square-metre house uses recyclable materials throughout, and incorporates both new and established methods for the control and use of solar energy. The house's sustainable features include—low-energy use achieved by appropriate set back of main glazing to allow winter sun access and summer sun shading; all day sun that opens up to the kitchen/dining/family room;

super insulation and double-glazing; and tiled concrete floor with underfloor heating to main living areas. Energy efficiency is further achieved through natural cross-ventilation to the main living area, and solar-heated water with heat-pump backup (the pool acts as a 'dump' for surplus solar-heated water in summer, allowing for almost year-round solar-heated water).

The pool area and gardens are linked to the house through paved extensions of the main living area. They will, in time, become part of the whole as landscaping develops.

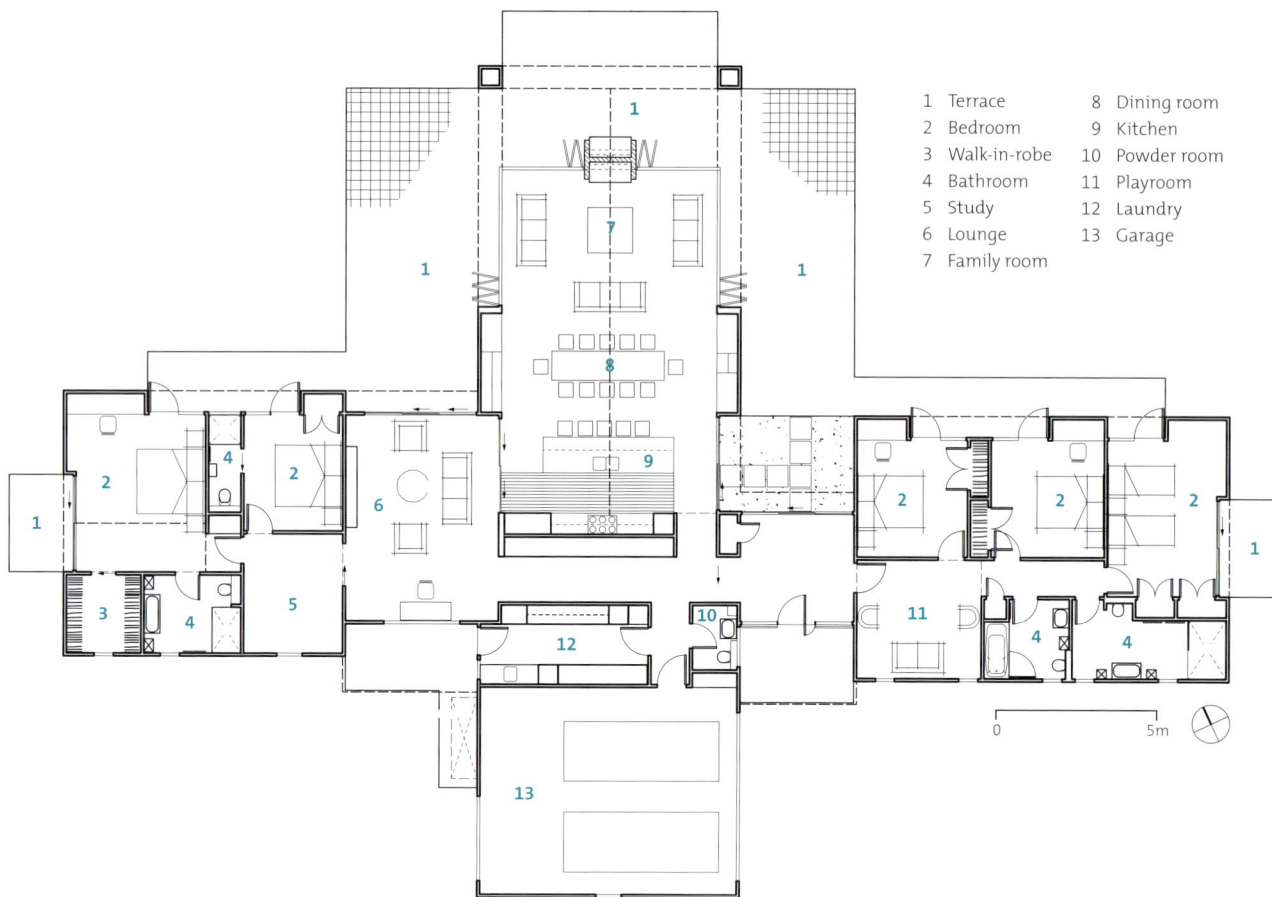

1	Terrace	8	Dining room
2	Bedroom	9	Kitchen
3	Walk-in-robe	10	Powder room
4	Bathroom	11	Playroom
5	Study	12	Laundry
6	Lounge	13	Garage
7	Family room		

0   5m

Ground floor

H1 House

Wooloowin, Queensland, Australia

Reddog Architects

Photography: Jon Linkins

H1 House seeks to break down the confines of a tight city block by promoting the concept of shared green space—the interrelation of and visual relationship between the house's living spaces, and the adjacent green space of neighbouring blocks.

The house was conceived as a long, low pavilion hovering above the ground plane, stretching from the street front to the rear boundary. Inverting a typical Queenslander arrangement, the house draws its circulation to the perimeter and unravels living spaces across the length of the site in a slender planning arrangement that promotes cross-ventilation and natural daylighting.

Expansive glazing and openings to the southern facade allow not only optimal day lighting, ventilation and outlook, but further creates a strong visual relationship and dialogue between the street and the house's living and circulation spaces. These living and circulation spaces are controlled by a large external curtain to the front deck. Large openings and a narrow planning arrangement—the house is generally only one-room deep—are conducive to cross-ventilation, while manually operable louvres allow the occupants to control the relative levels of air movement. High ceilings and high-level openings encourage air movement in living spaces. The house also exhibits sustainable features such as photovoltaics for power supply and a tank for rainwater collection.

1 Carport
2 Utility
3 Bedroom
4 Bathroom
5 Kitchen
6 Deck
7 Dining room
8 Library
9 Living room
10 Ensuite
11 Walk-in-robe

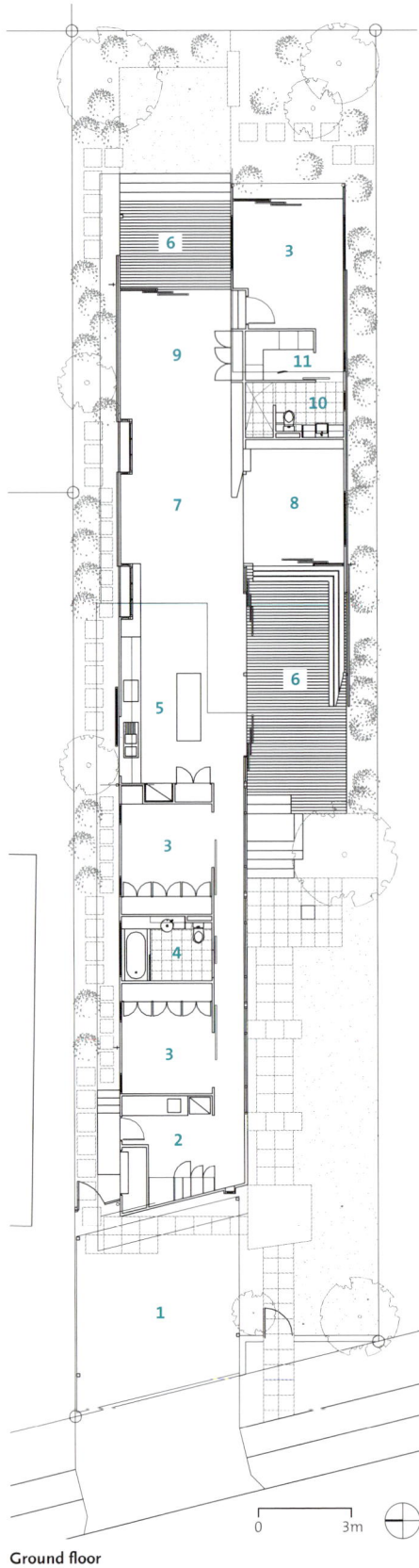

Ground floor

0   3m

Highgate Hill

Brisbane, Queensland, Australia

Richard Kirk Architect

Photography: Patrick Bingham-Hall,
Jon Linkins

The Highgate Hill residence is located on a south-facing ravine. The steepness of the rectangular site has resulted in a verdant and mature landscape consisting of a mixture of natives and exotics, which created the opportunity to place the house within a rich landscape environment. As a result of the steepness of the site and the desire to connect the house to an outdoor ground plane, the house adopts two distinct identities—the north (landscape) and east (street).

The rectangular form of the house is organised over three levels, with the middle level containing living and dining spaces and also the point of entry from the street. The upper level contains all the bedrooms and a void that is located over the dining area. The lower level contains a guest room and a media space. The void within the house acts not only as a spatial device to orient and extenuate the verticality of the tall trees outside, but also separates parent and children's bedrooms. The stair is an important organisational reference between the levels and is treated as a sculptural element that twists slightly within the void to allow its form to visually link all levels.

In response to the dominance of the landscape, the house is entirely clad in timber and uses timber glazed facade systems where each species is selected to age in response to its orientation and weathering.

1 Bedroom
2 Bathroom
3 Robe
4 Powder room
5 Void

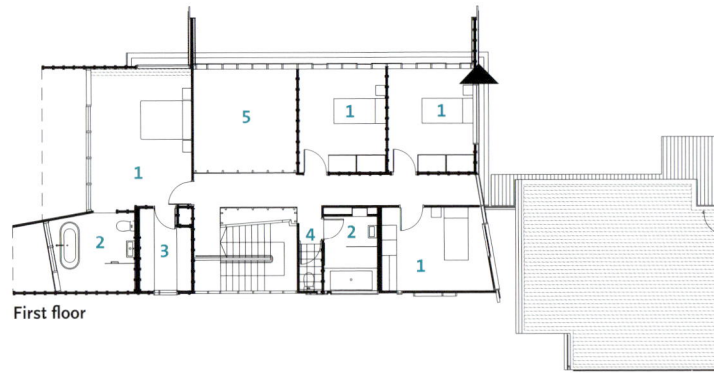

First floor

1 Entry
2 Kitchen
3 Dining room
4 Living room
5 Study
6 Laundry
7 Store
8 Powder room
9 Carport
10 Swimming pool
11 Lawn
12 Deck

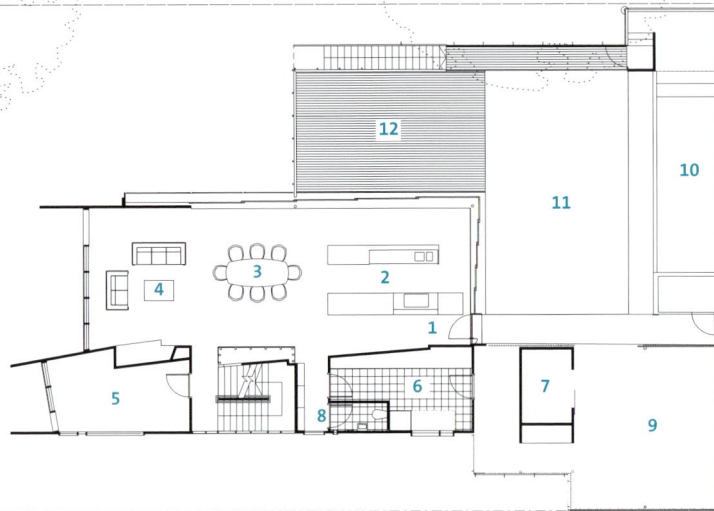

Ground floor

1 Playroom
2 Bedroom
3 Bathroom
4 Deck

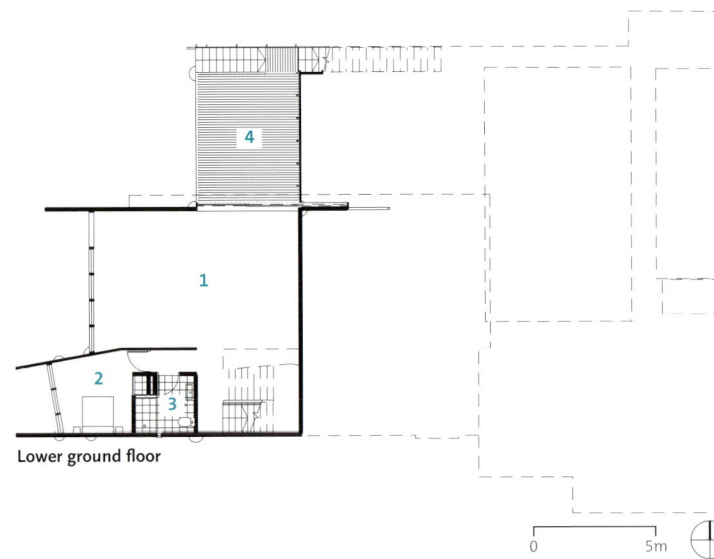

Lower ground floor

0   5m

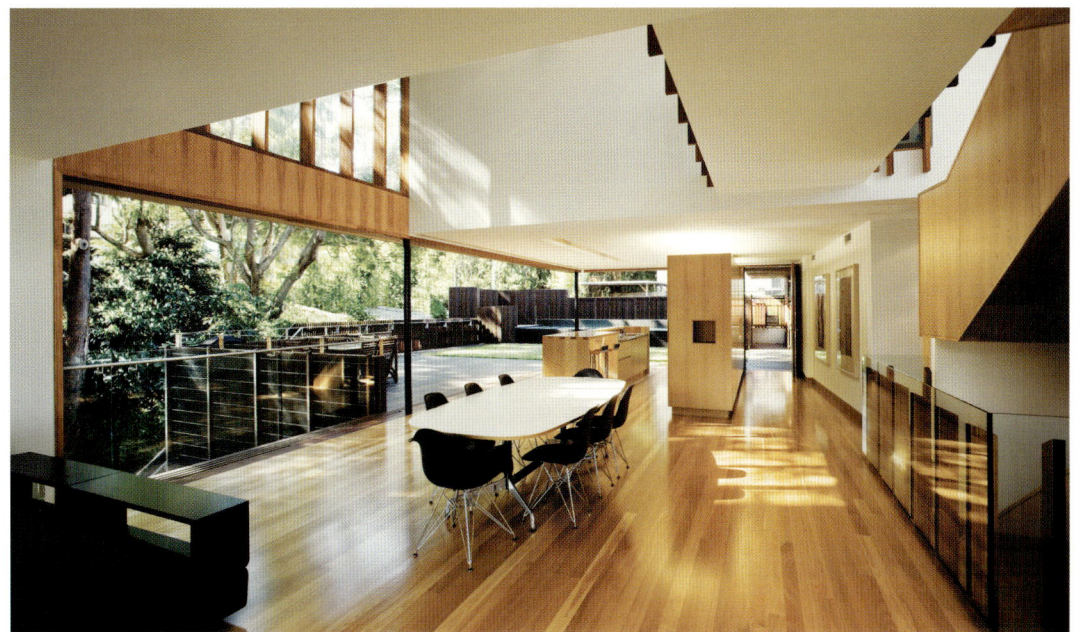

Leigh House

Omaha Bay, North Island, New Zealand

Tennent + Brown Architects

Photography: Paul McCredie

The site sits above the entrance to Leigh Harbour with a view toward Little Barrier Island. There are intimate views from the site back into Leigh Harbour. The site was previously occupied by a small old cottage, which was a local landmark to the harbour entrance.

The clients required a house for their family of four, designed to allow both to work from home, one having private clients visit the house for appointments. They desired the house to be very private, and to have a tower and space for yoga sessions.

The house is imagined as slipping up out of the cliff, as one strata moving against another. The weathered Lawson's cypress-cladding was chosen to silver with time and merge with the trees surrounding the property. The house is envisioned as being part of the cliff.

This same idea is carried over to how one moves around inside the house, slipping through spaces, compressed in places and in others released. The 'inscrutable' nature of the house was not to discover all in one glance, to not be able to predict how the house unfolds.

Sustainable features include: gas used for underfloor heating and cooking to minimise electricity use, evacuated-tube solar water heating, rainwater collection, reuse of grey water through sewerage dispersal system, sustainably-harvested Lawson's cypress wall-cladding, recycled kauri floorboards, recycled door, and predominantly fluorescent lighting throughout.

1	Garage	8	Work room
2	Study	9	Bedroom
3	Winter garden	10	Bathroom
4	Living room	11	Dressing room
5	Kitchen	12	Library
6	Meals area	13	Store room
7	Veranda	14	Tower

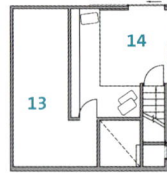

Second floor

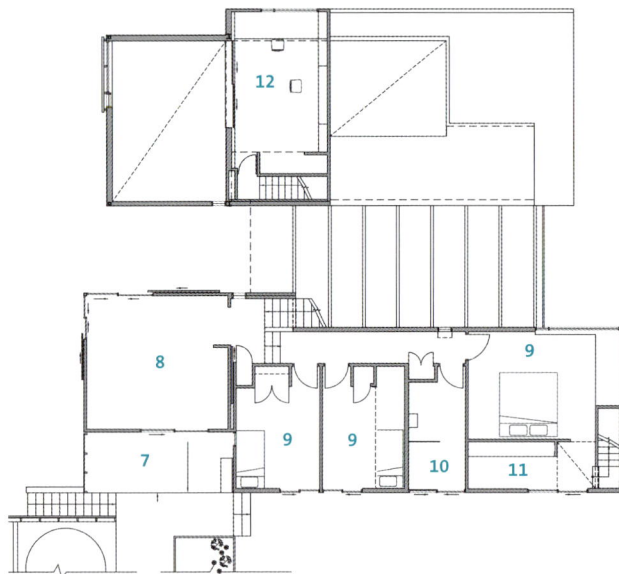

First floor

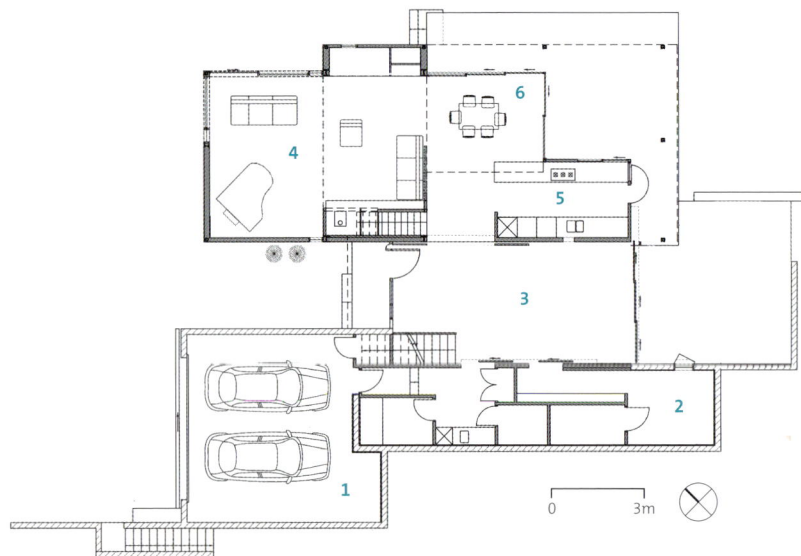

Ground floor

0   3m

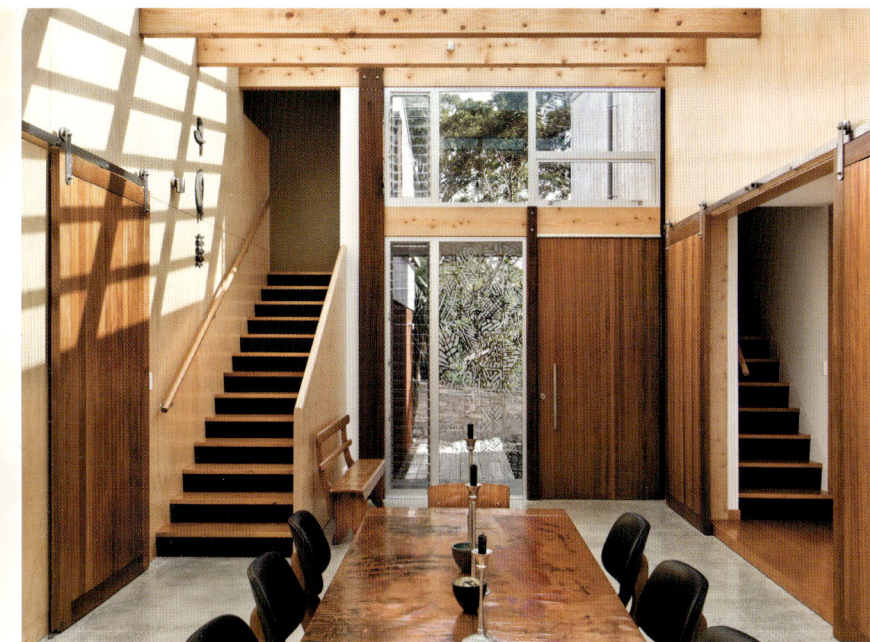

Lethlean House

Metung, Victoria, Australia

Craig Rossetti Architects

Photography: Andrew Ashton

Lethlean House is a holiday house designed to give urban visitors an experience that contrasts dramatically with their usual environment.

As the house is only accessible by boat, building materials are by necessity lightweight. Construction was carried out in an expressed local vernacular form. Timber is exposed in the floor construction to express the constructivist nature of self-build. The pitched roofs give drama to the composition but also hark back to the shack. Delicate slats are incorporated to create a new version of the transitionary veranda space. The timber is left untreated to revert to the silver-grey of the surrounding landscape.

The informality of the holiday shack is promoted by the visitor being taken directly into the outdoor living area on arrival, not to a formal front door. The progression through the building is to the shared children's bunkroom, which terminates the axis. Progression into the living space via a reduced-height corridor explodes out with an increased height and a skewed 'box-in' plan and elevation, drawing the water and bush views into the house.

The building is completely 'off grid', further enhancing the holiday house experience. Power is produced through solar cells on the roof, hot water through solar heaters.

All these elements combine to give the occupants a more comprehensive understanding of their locale and to provide them with an experience truly different to their city existence.

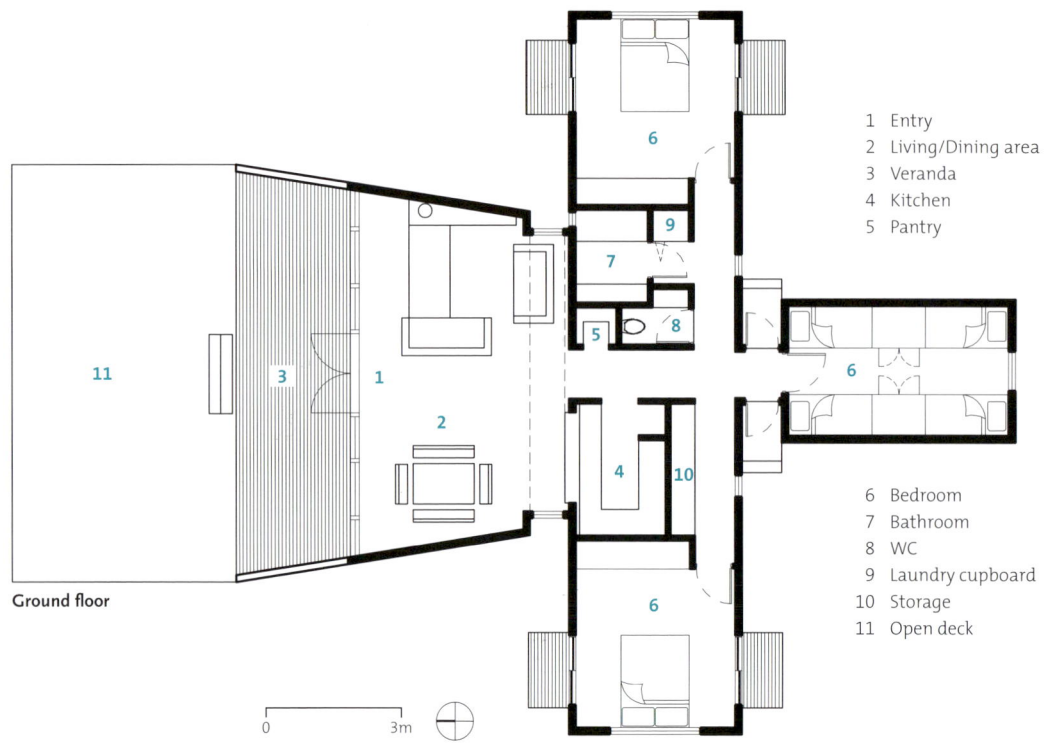

Ground floor

1 Entry
2 Living/Dining area
3 Veranda
4 Kitchen
5 Pantry

6 Bedroom
7 Bathroom
8 WC
9 Laundry cupboard
10 Storage
11 Open deck

0   3m

Lockyer House

Bardon, Queensland, Australia

Shaun Lockyer Architects with Arkhefield

Photography: Scott Burrows
(Aperture Photography)

Lockyer House is a small, contemporary extension to a post-war house in Bardon, a leafy and hilly fringe suburb in Brisbane. The design looks to address the primary architectural issues of context and language, as well as finding the 'essence' of what is needed from an accommodation/resource perspective in an effort to create an engaging but practical and economical outcome.

The design of this house is all about creation of a simple, cost-effective 'pod' that needed to accommodate the needs of a young family that had outgrown the original cottage. The other core function of the extension was to improve the connection to the landscape, engage with the sky and to provide a more climatically comfortable place to live, using the minimum resources possible to achieve this. Essentially, the space is about joy.

The retention of the old cottage preserves cultural and architectural identity and, more basically, public expectation. The contemporary extension, while highly visible from the street, is partly concealed by the large tree on the site and gives over the landscape zone to the public realm. The house is highly animated at night, forming a 'lantern' that creates a sense of joy in the street for all.

Section

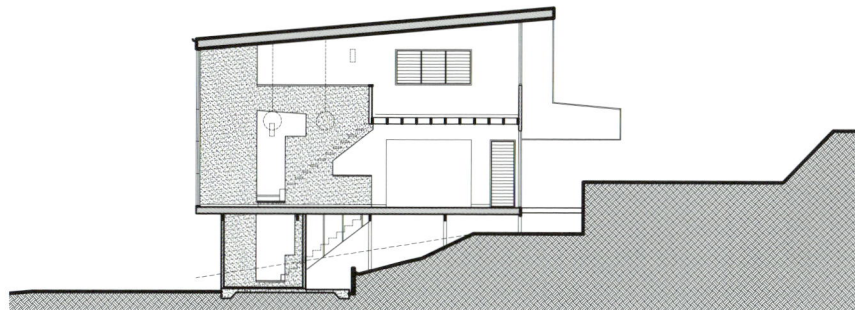

1 Store room
2 Entry
3 Garage
4 Store room
5 Rumpus room
6 Pool
7 Family room
8 Kitchen
9 Living room
10 Dining room
11 Outdoor living area
12 Bedroom
13 Ensuite
14 Bathroom
15 Laundry

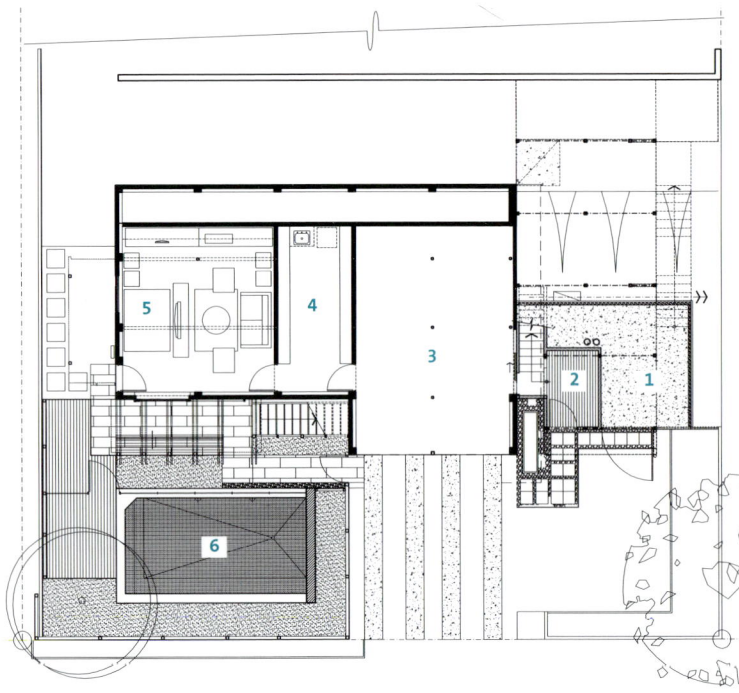

Ground floor

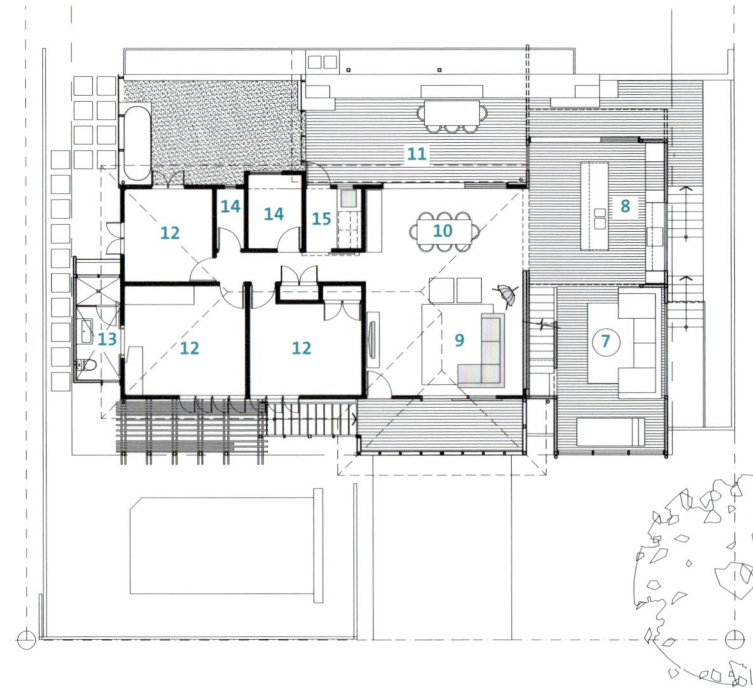

First floor

0   5m

Mooramie House

Sydney, NSW, Australia

Tobias Partners

Photography: Justin Alexander

The mass, proportion and simple architectural expression of this new 2-storey rear addition is sympathetic and respectful to the existing Federation-style cottage. The relatively simple form of the rear addition, situated below the ridgeline of the existing building, allows for the original house to remain the dominant feature of the site, thereby minimising the impact to its heritage significance.

The new–old exterior connection is delineated by the expressed shadow-line created by the junction of the flush recessed steel frame of the new addition. Similarly, the new and old components have been matched in the same paint colour. The visual impact of the new southern wall has been reduced through the creation of an elevated garden that internally houses the amenities block, including butler's pantry, laundry and pool WC.

Oversized timber-framed sliding doors on a travertine-stone inlay track pocket away to enable a single interior–exterior space with a continuous travertine floor finish. External hardwood-timber screens to the first-floor windows provide privacy as well as shelter from the sun. A restrained palette of natural materials forms the basis of the interior fit-out, including recycled timber flooring and travertine-stone floors.

Links between the lower and upper levels of the new house have been achieved through spatial devices that include the living room void, which is articulated through a new double-height northern window with timber screen-over, and an adjacent interior double-height grasscloth wall.

1   Existing carport
2   Bathroom
3   Bedroom
4   Patio
5   Guest bedroom
6   Study
7   Lounge
8   Powder room
9   Cellar
10 Living room
11 Pantry
12 WC
13 Laundry
14 Kitchen
15 Dining room
16 Outdoor kitchen
17 Terrace
18 Pool
19 Study
20 Walk-in-robe
21 Balcony

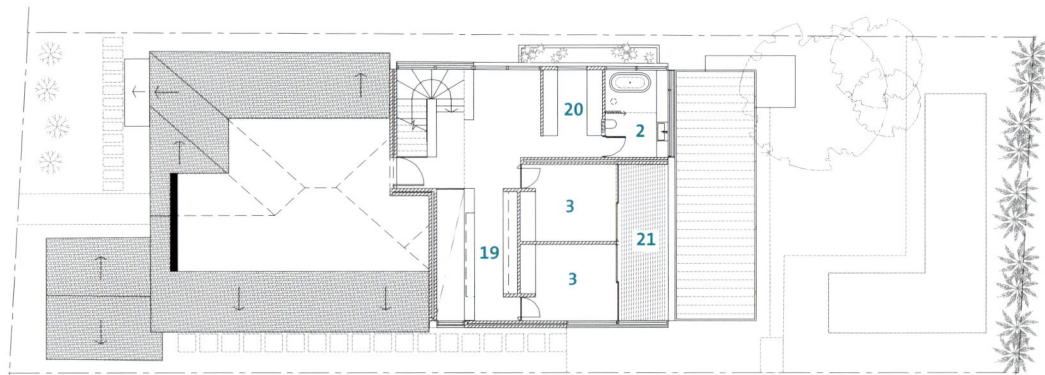

First floor

0   5m

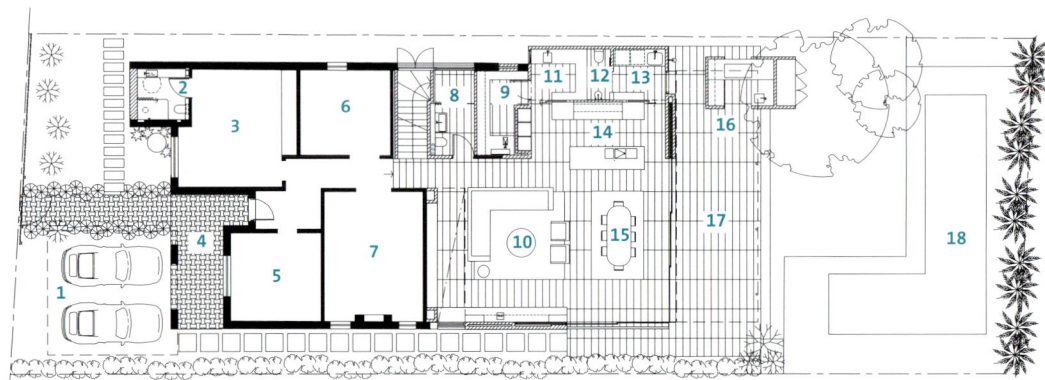

Ground floor

Muldrock House

Kewarra Beach, Queensland, Australia

Circa 2000 Architecture and
Construction

Photography: Brad Newton

The Muldrock House site is battle-axe in shape, with existing houses on two sides and a wetland reserve dominated by pandanus trees on the third side. This natural wetland is the main focus of the home, not only for its beauty but also for its use as a shelter from the climate.

Budget constraints led to an innovative structure with as many pre-ordered elements as possible, which were then assembled on site. The resulting lightweight structure is climatically appropriate and sustainable. Being 'post-and-beam' in nature, it allows the house to be easily modified and adapted to suit the needs of various occupiers over time.

For a house to be 'sustainable' in the tropics it must promote passive cooling. The Muldrock House is oriented towards prevailing breezes, and is further ventilated via convection through the use of clerestory louvre windows. The lack of internal walls also promotes the free flow of air through the house, though spaces within the house are still able to be delineated via the use of split levels and mezzanines. The house is also elevated above ground level to allow the flow of cooling air beneath the flooring.

The building is not pretentious; rather, it connects with the environment. It sits at the end of a suburban court and, while appearing 'different' to the surrounding houses, it is not out of place. The aesthetics are carefully resolved to balance architectural ambition with environmental conscience.

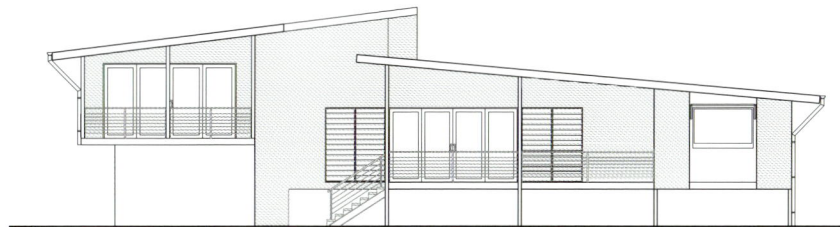

Elevation

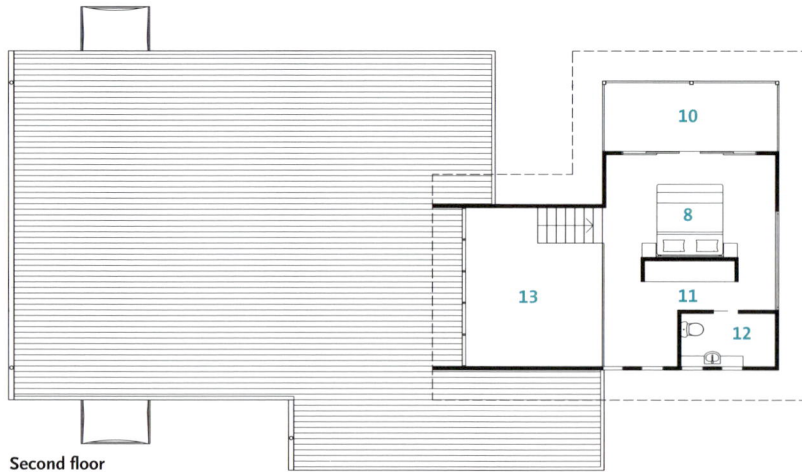

Second floor

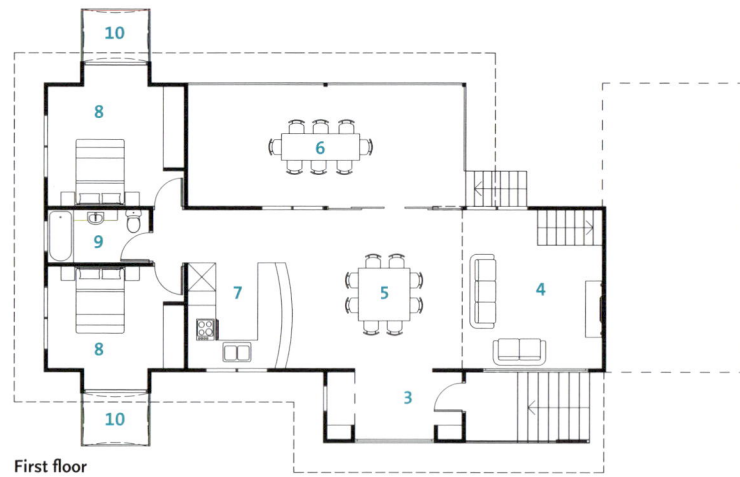

First floor

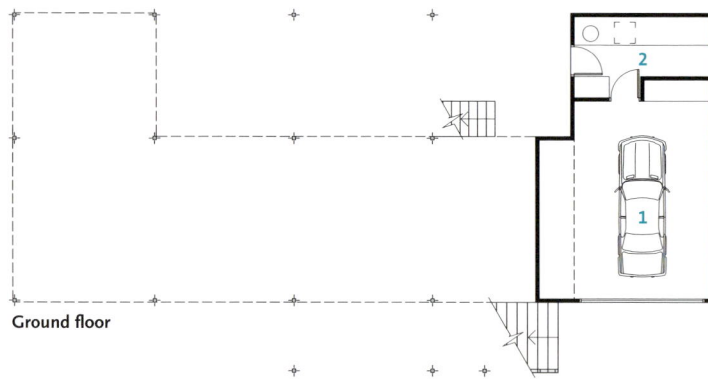

Ground floor

1	Garage	8	Bedroom
2	Laundry	9	Bathroom
3	Entry	10	Balcony
4	Living room	11	Walk-in-robe
5	Dining room	12	Ensuite
6	Outdoor living area	13	Void
7	Kitchen		

0   3m

N+C Townhouse

Geelong, Victoria, Australia

Studio 101 Architects

Photography: Trevor Mein

Once occupied by a dilapidated dwelling, this new residence explores how contemporary, sustainable architecture can rest peacefully with heritage neighbours. The split-level residence follows the natural topography of the site and leads one along a continuous walkway of recycled timber before opening to the double-height northern living zone. This central spine through the linear pavilion also links the internal and external spaces through a system of pivoting, sliding and louvred screens.

A central courtyard allows the house to breathe, and provides varying degrees of openness and intimacy, light, and fresh air. Sustainable living solutions include double-glazed windows with argon gas, rainwater harvested into a series of underground tanks, grey water reused for irrigation, while recycled timber and low-VOC coatings are used extensively.

The overt expression of the recycled-timber structural system forms a refined portal frame that is expressed both internally and externally. Inspired by traditional heritage houses of the region, a balance of materials including masonry and a lightweight skin of timber weatherboards were incorporated. This all contributed to a finely-crafted design response, providing a sense of honesty in structure and materials and, ultimately, serenity in the urban landscape.

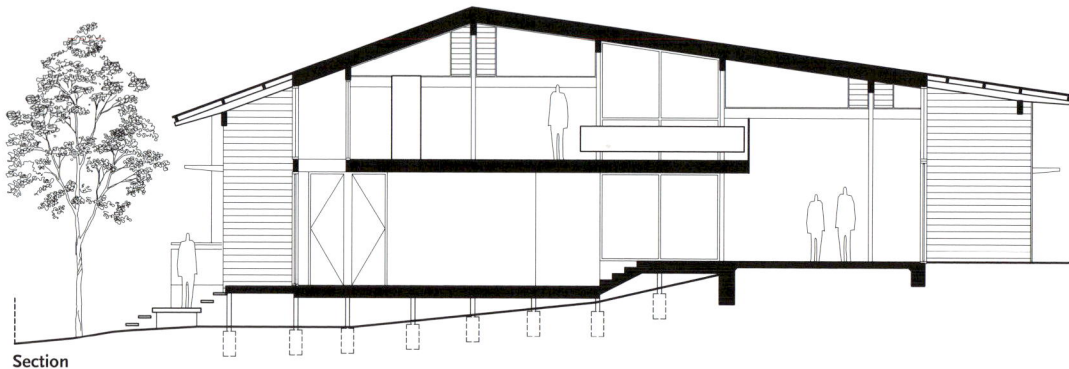

Section

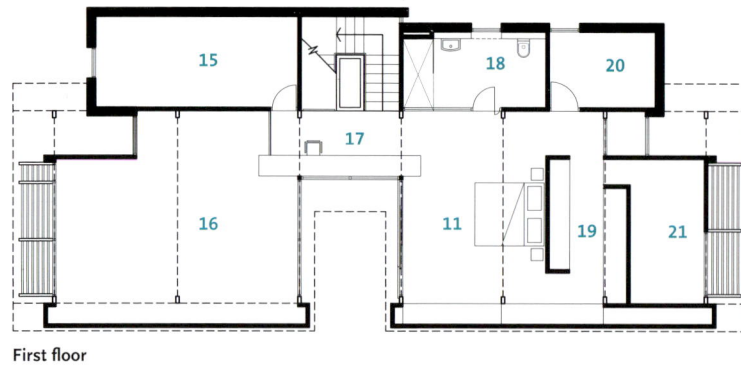

First floor

1 Water feature
2 Terrace
3 Living area
4 Kitchen
5 Pantry
6 Dining area
7 Courtyard
8 Laundry
9 Play room
10 Powder room
11 Bedroom
12 Entry
13 Bathroom
14 Entry deck
15 Store room
16 Void
17 Study
18 Ensuite
19 Walk-in-robe
20 Gym
21 Art room

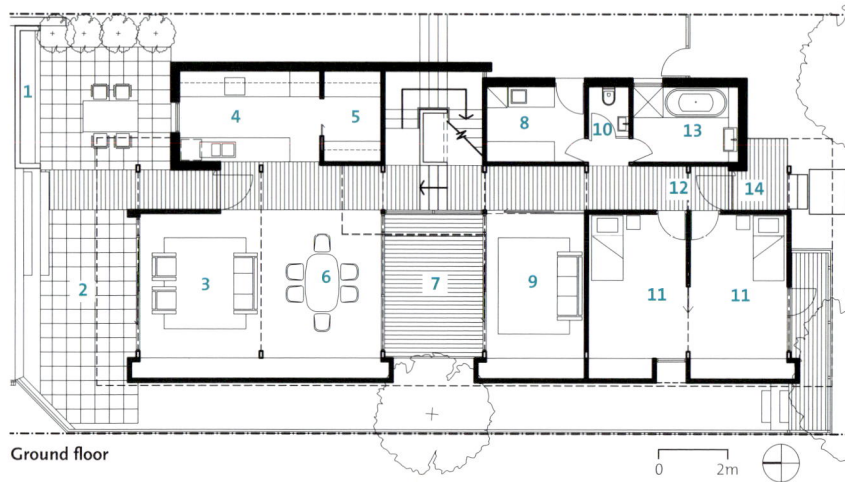

Ground floor

0 2m

Newtown House

Newtown, NSW, Australia

Sam Crawford Architects

Photography: Brett Boardman

The client's brief for this project prioritised quality of light, functionality and an honest expression of materials. The result is a robust construction that will outlive the memory of its cost.

A single sculptural staircase weaves together the three levels, from a heavy concrete base to a luminous platform of steel and glass. Aside from a single glass sheet that replaces the original tiled front porch, the building skin and its relationship to the street and rear lane remain. With the exception of the front portion of the basement, which is hollowed out for the kitchen, all rooms are left intact.

In order to suit the living patterns of a young family with two small children, the lower level is now a light, open, continuous living platform. Utilities are set to one side and sheathed in glass. Raw concrete, timber, steel and glass provide each level with a distinct feel.

Bespoke 'black' steel hardware, door jambs, stair treads and handrails clearly evidence their on-site fabrication. Hardwood joists from the existing terrace are reused in new joinery. The form-ply from construction of concrete elements has been reworked into textured door panels for the cellar.

Natural and raw materials, 'black' steel, hardwood and glass, requiring little or no surface finish, are used throughout. Components such as the stainless-steel stair rigging and hardware for the glass walls were selected for superior quality. Each element is designed and built to last, reducing future waste.

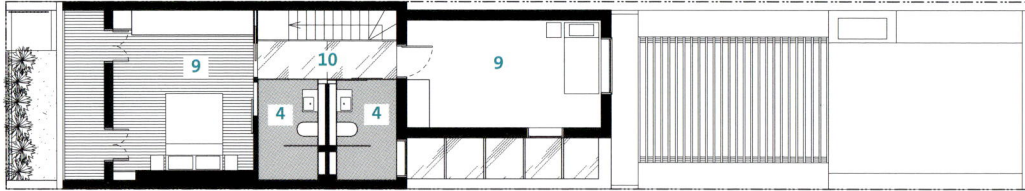

First floor

1 Kitchen
2 Dining room
3 Living room
4 Bathroom
5 Laundry
6 Pantry
7 Wine cellar
8 Music room
9 Bedroom
10 Glass
11 Pergola

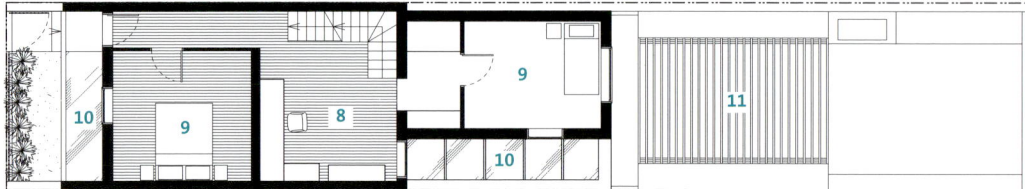

Ground floor

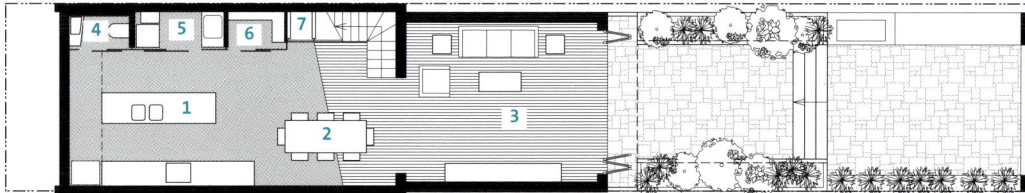

Lower ground floor

0   5m

Nicholson Parade

Mac-Interactive Architects

Photography: Richard Glover

This extensive renovation of a 1970s brick house in Cronulla contributes to contemporary interior design practice in its re-use of an existing building, adapted and modified to suit the changing needs of its long-standing owners.

The client brief for a robust, easy-to-maintain palette was met with natural materials and carefully crafted connections. The material palette and its detailing was reduced to bare essentials, helping the spaces form a backdrop for the colourful lives of the clients. Materials were chosen on the basis of their intrinsic character, lower embodied energy and ability to age gracefully.

After a complete strip out, the building received a clarified zoning of upper-level living, mid-level sleeping and downstairs creative retreats—all hanging off a clear axis. The upstairs is a theatre for the ever-changing light of Gunnamatta Bay beyond. Large horizontal window openings capture the horizon line and spectacular sunsets across the water. The eastern roof is punctured by a simple and clean square which allows the morning sun to track across the floor. After dusk, a mix of illumination from a perimeter lighting shelf, and incidental lighting offer opportunities for night-time ambience.

Housing more intimate creative spaces, the lower level connects to the rear garden, decks and swimming pool with a hallway library containing a memory of the previous plan, etched on the sandblasted concrete ceiling. Entry to the poetry and music studios is via openings in the bookcase, a symbolic departure from the everyday.

First floor

1 Entry
2 Dining room
3 Living room
4 Kitchen
5 Balcony
6 Bedroom
7 Garage
8 Music room
9 Library
10 Study
11 Laundry/Bathroom
12 External deck area

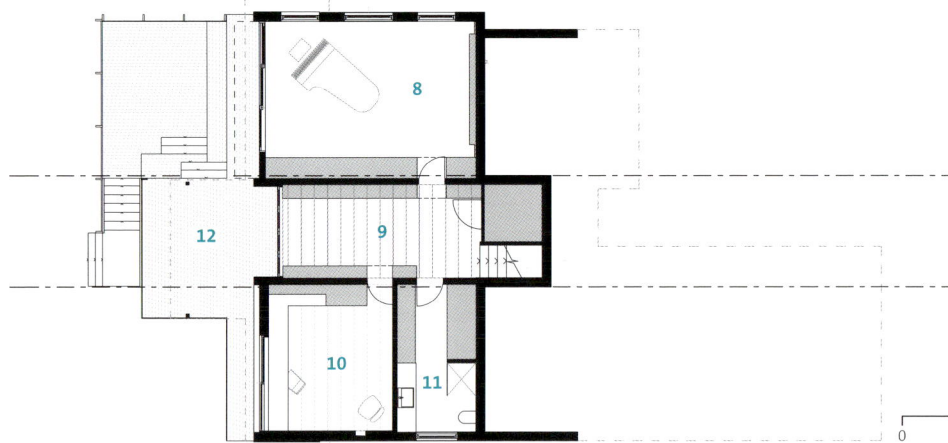

Ground floor

0   4m

Northpoint Residence

Kingscliff, NSW, Australia

Scott Carpenter Architect

Photography: Brent Middleton

Nestled comfortably behind the dunes and enjoying panoramic ocean views from Cape Byron to the Queensland border, the Northpoint Residence is a great example of 21st-century architecture providing a relaxing sanctuary where the owners escape the stress of a hectic profession and immerse themselves in a casual beachside lifestyle.

The real challenge was to create an elegant and timeless home, robust enough to withstand the rigours of the harsh seaside environment, exude a bold contemporary confidence yet maintain a cosy, comfortable and homely feel. A strong sense of entry was paramount, as were generosity of space and the capturing of views. The home must open up and engage with the adjacent parklands and passers-by but also adapt to provide privacy when required.

The strong vertical elements and sleek horizontal lines are delicately balanced and softened by a varied textural palette of concrete, stone, weatherboards and chunky weathered timber. Sleek frameless glass balustrades and fine stainless-steel handrails make way for the crisp white rendered exo-skeletal structure of the verandas and roof lines while, in contrast, the rugged stone chimney connects the floors and anchors the structure. Internally, sleek fixtures and polished-concrete floors balance the recycled hardwood floorboards.

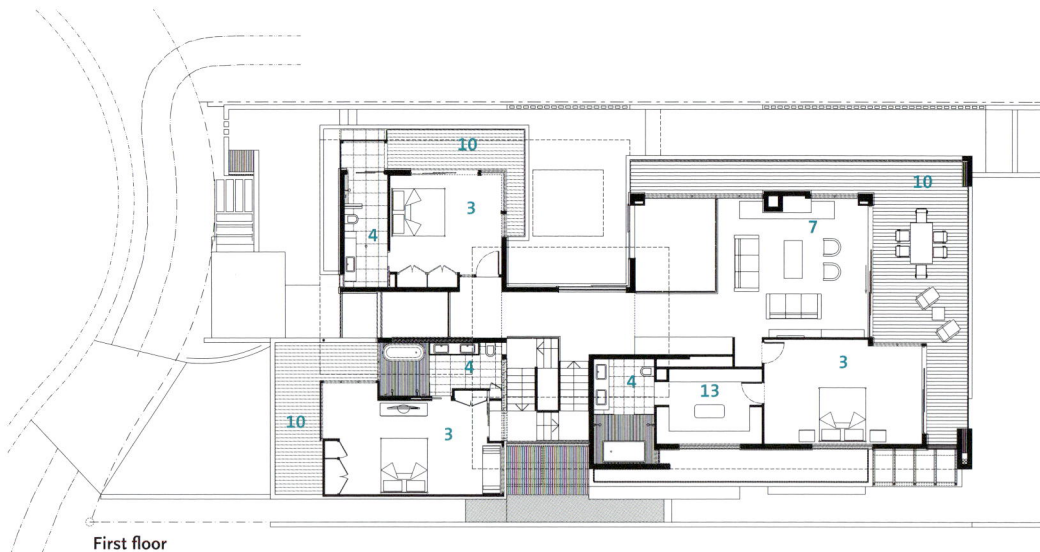

First floor

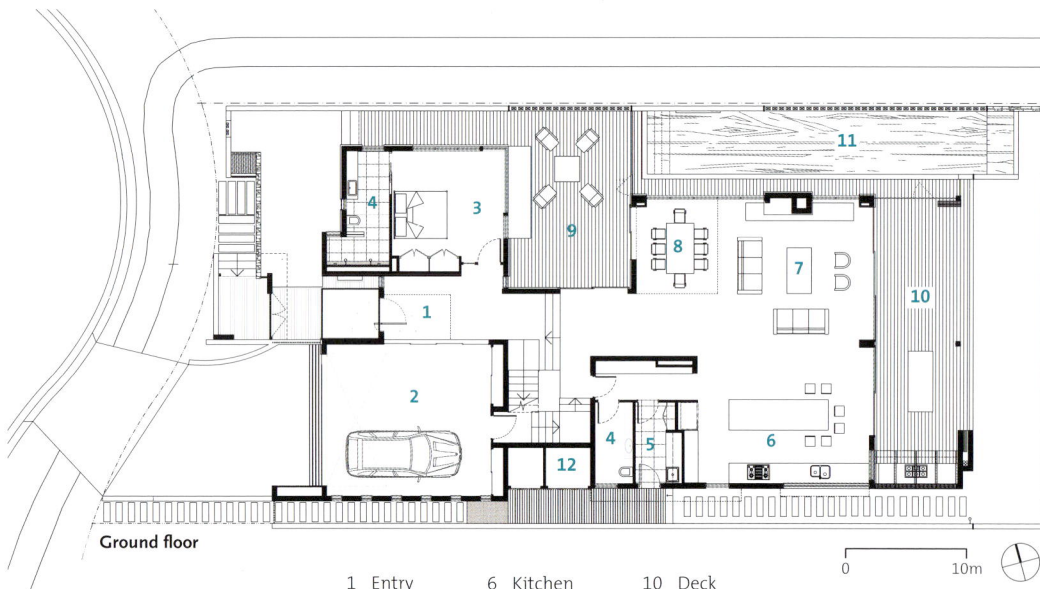

Ground floor

0   10m

1	Entry	6	Kitchen	10	Deck
2	Garage	7	Living room	11	Lap pool
3	Bedroom	8	Dining room	12	Beach store
4	Bathroom	9	Courtyard	13	Dressing room
5	Laundry				

Outlook Residence

Bardon, Queensland, Australia

Phorm Architecture + Design

Photography: Camera Obscura

The Outlook Residence is a considered set of additions and reworking of an existing house set in the established suburb of Bardon. Primary to this project is the 'mapping of light', installed as a precursive design agent, modulating the plan, section and program allocation, eventually scribing many of the project's ideas and details.

Internal light cores were prompted by a pragmatic requirement to deliver light to the floor below, and driven by concerns of disconnection between lives throughout the house through 'stratification' of the plans. The threshold between the two ages of the house are bled with light and linked with incised forms of plasterwork to produce a seamless whole.

The house is also formally responsive to the presence and scale of majestic jacarandas in the neighbours' yards. One tree is paired with a vertical element, a white tower—grounding the original structure—and a series of conversations have ensued through the design.

The intention and response at Outlook focused on providing a young family with a joyous house, one which will manage the changes and demands through their maturity, and one filled with delight and discourse.

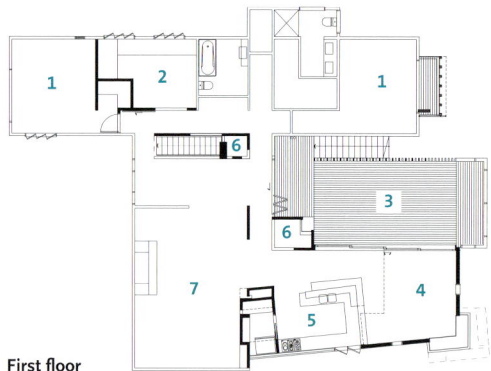

First floor

1 Bedroom
2 Study
3 Deck
4 Family room
5 Kitchen
6 Light
7 Living room

Ground floor

1 Store room
2 Cabana
3 Pool
4 Rumpus room
5 Light
6 Bedroom
7 Courtyard
8 Bathroom
9 Laundry
10 Cellar

0   5m

Oxlade House

New Farm, Queensland, Australia

Arkhefield

Photography: Scott Burrows
(Aperture Photography)

Oxlade House explores the idea of a singular graphic form extruded and stepped along a narrow inner-suburban site. The internal spaces are captured by a boldly-sloped rear concrete wall and steel roof. These elements create an armature to the rear, while the full northern frontage visually and physically extends out into the external living spaces.

While unapologetically contemporary in its expression, the house is an abstraction of traditional housing typologies of a legible expressive roof form capping a grounded heavy-weight base. A finer palette of crafted screening and cladding materials made from copper, timber and steel add texture and detail to soften the forms. An uncluttered, open planning arrangement maintains the clarity of the dynamic section internally and allows the focus to remain on the outdoor living areas.

The provision of a filtered veranda to an elevated living room along the street frontage ensures an engagement with the street is maintained despite the sequestered environment created beyond the garden wall. The adjoining living room envelope is conceived as one generous space punctuated by a few key sculptural building elements.

While the design is bold and distinctive, the house also functions as a comfortable and robust family home. The use of natural materials and crafted detailing contribute to a relaxed, liveable environment that engages the outdoor living areas with all spaces.

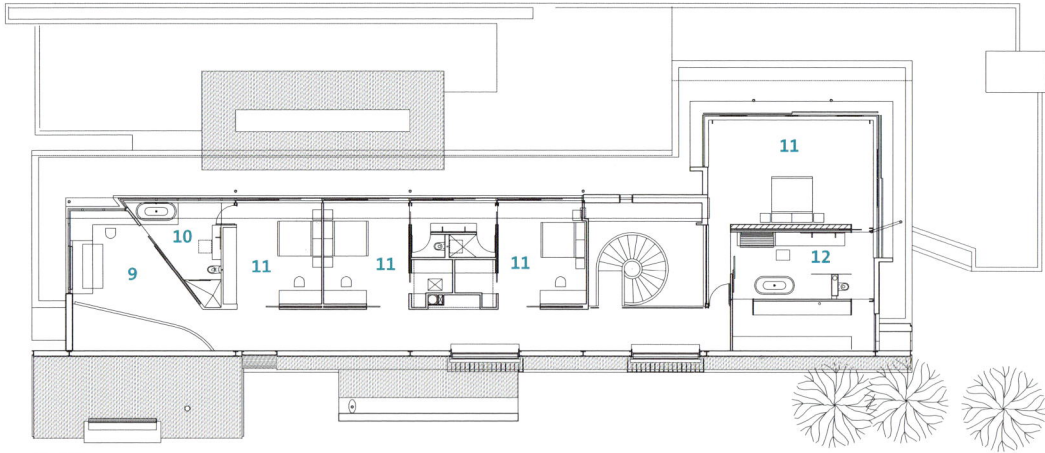

First floor

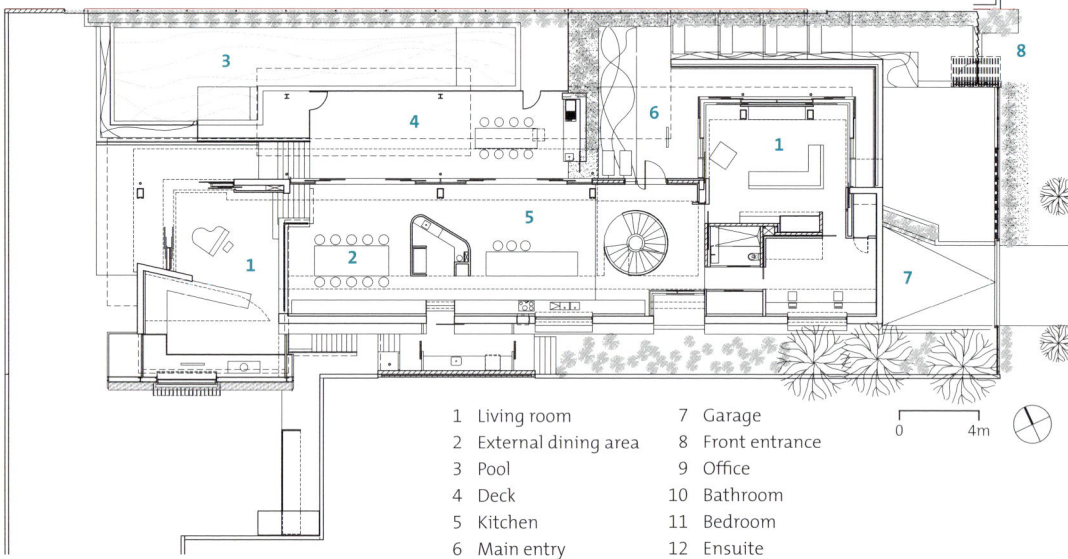

Ground floor

1	Living room	7	Garage
2	External dining area	8	Front entrance
3	Pool	9	Office
4	Deck	10	Bathroom
5	Kitchen	11	Bedroom
6	Main entry	12	Ensuite

0   4m

Perforated House

Brunswick, Victoria, Australia

Kavellaris Urban Design

Photography: Peter Bennetts

The Perforated House project is a critique on cultural attitudes and how they are determined; a critique on what is considered to be of heritage significance and how to narrate such ideas in a critical and contemporary manner.

Are the symbolism and the idea more important than the architectural consequence?

The strategy was to break down the elements of the terrace house, and to critique and respond. The main areas of investigation were symbolism and ornamentation, the public/private realm and redefining its boundaries, solar orientation, environmental sustainability and programming of the plan. The 'idea' and the 'symbolism' of the terrace were to be retained, but elevating the gesture to an ironic or even satirical level to engage in a public debate.

The house was to be more than just a facade or a graphic on a building paying tribute to Venturi's 'decorated shed'; instead, the external facade can be experienced internally and is also a multifunctional device that constantly transforms the built form from solid to void, from private to public, from opaque to translucent. The operable wall, or the absence of the facade, confronts the notion of a house being a static object.

The use of operable walls, doors, curtains and glass walls enables the occupants to change the experience and environment. This architectural manipulation of space blurs the boundaries between inside and outside, the public and private realm.

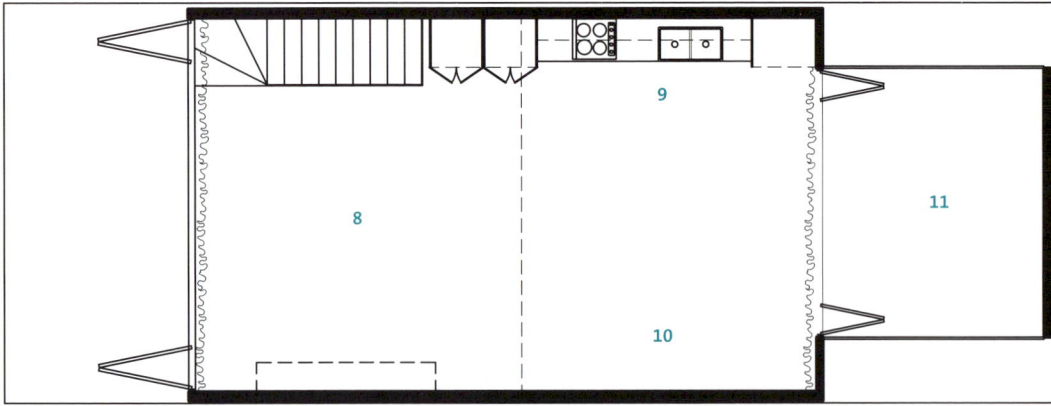

First floor

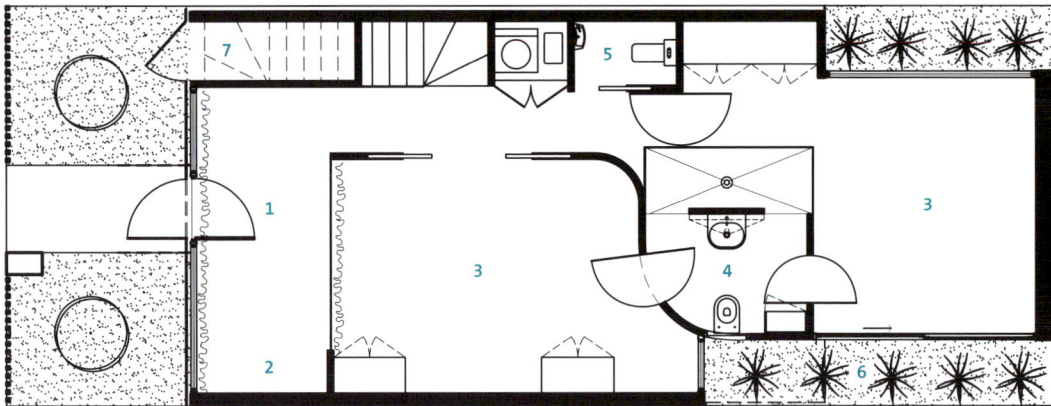

Ground floor

1	Entry foyer	5	Powder room	9	Kitchen	
2	Study	6	Courtyard	10	Dining room	
3	Bedroom	7	Store room	11	Backyard	
4	Ensuite	8	Living room			

0   2m

Point Lonsdale House

Point Lonsdale, Victoria, Australia

Kathryn Robson Architecture

Photography: Lisa Cohen Photography

This rural residence is situated on a flat site an hour out of Melbourne. The house consists of a massive, linear rammed earth spine, enhanced by the contrasting timber walls. Key views into the courtyard and decking spaces are enjoyed from all bedrooms and living areas, with the master bedroom benefiting from a private internal garden with sliding screens to provide privacy from the public courtyard when desired. The low, desert style landscaping provides a green space that requires little or no water and maintenance, and allows the oversized presence of the rammed earth walls to be felt.

The house turns its back from the street, allowing the focus to be on the internal courtyard rather than the neighbours. The exterior elevation creates an almost monastic facade of two 3-metre-high rammed earth walls. The rammed earth walls provide good thermal mass, and all windows and doors are double glazed. The roof has deep overhangs to the north and east, with minimal western windows, ensuring the summer sun is kept at bay. This, along with the passive cooling from the high openable western and eastern windows, minimises the need for air conditioning. The overhanging roof, high openable windows, and thick rammed earth walls all result in an ecologically responsible building that remains at a fairly constant temperature.

1 Garage
2 External entry
3 Internal entry
4 Bedroom
5 Walk-in-robe/Ensuite
6 Study
7 Bathroom

8 Laundry
9 Kitchen
10 Living room
11 Outdoor living
12 Outdoor kitchen
13 Pool

Ground floor

0   5m

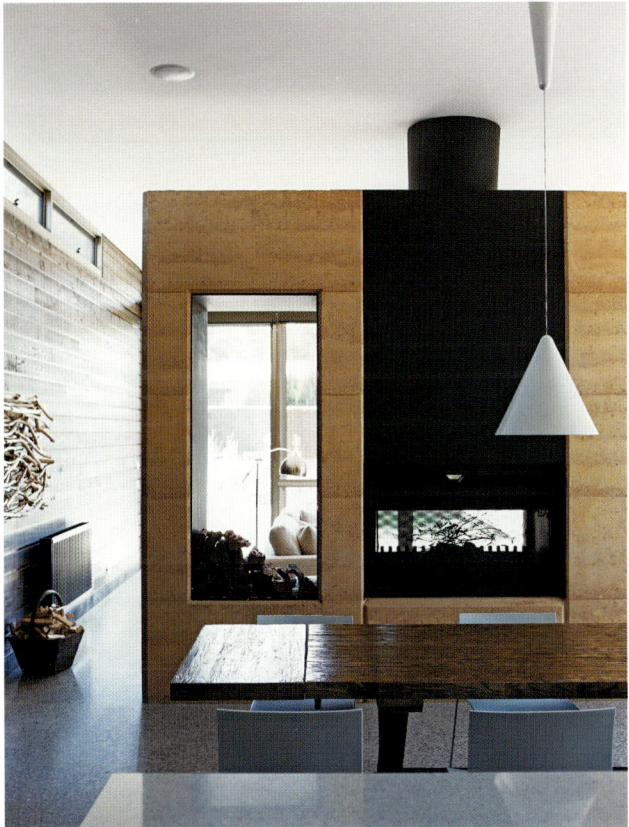

Quigley House

Cairns, Queensland, Australia

Circa 2000 Architecture and Construction

Photography: Brad Newton

Quigley House is built on the edge of a magnificent tropical creek in Clifton Beach, Far North Queensland. Refined design principles suited to the tropical environment were required to integrate the house with its surroundings.

To meet the budget it was necessary to produce an innovative structure made up of as many pre-ordered elements as possible, to be assembled on site. The final structure evolved into a clever mix of innovative and sustainable materials. To give the form of the building texture and interest, the 'Mechano kit' structure is exposed, thus avoiding the need to add decorative elements to the building as a false facade.

A clear goal was set to incorporate as many sustainable design principles as possible, combined with key tropical design principles—the promotion of cooling breezes, ventilation by convection, reducing the radiation of heat, and the sheltering of walls and openings.

The dominant feature of the house is the relationship between the internal environment and the tropical climate. Quigley House is a true 'inside–outside' house that acknowledges the elements, allowing the occupants to enjoy the ever-changing tropical climate.

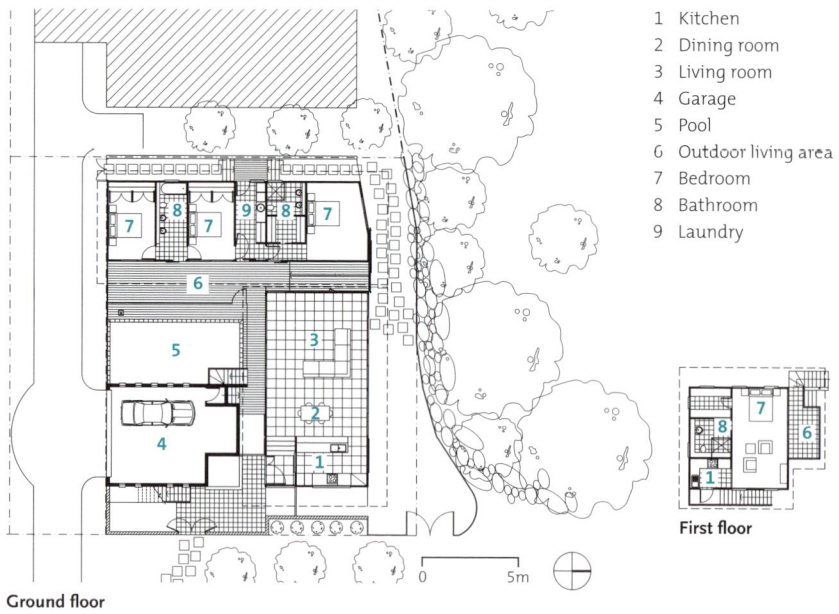

Ground floor

1 Kitchen
2 Dining room
3 Living room
4 Garage
5 Pool
6 Outdoor living area
7 Bedroom
8 Bathroom
9 Laundry

First floor

Randwick House

Randwick, NSW, Australia

Cullinan Ivanov Partnership

Photography: Giles Westley

Randwick House, located opposite a small park in Randwick, is situated within the North Randwick Heritage Conservation Area.

The brief called for a four-bedroom house with an open-plan living/dining/kitchen area that needed to have a connection to outdoor entertaining and a new swimming pool. The design solution was to extend to the rear and keep the existing house as a single-storey Federation cottage. The addition was designed to provide a clear separation between the original house and the new work.

The living/dining/kitchen area is located in the extended rear of the house, while the original house contains the bedrooms and bathrooms. The new addition is defined by an off-form concrete roof supported by steel columns, which have been incorporated into the glazing system in order to make them 'disappear'. The roof is punctured by four skylight openings that track the movement of the sun throughout the day. This open-plan space flows to an outdoor timber deck from which the pool is accessed via four steps. The roof floats past the glazed doors to create an overhang and provide sun control to the north in summer.

1   Kitchen
2   Dining room
3   Living room
4   Study
5   Bedroom
6   Bathroom
7   Deck
8   BBQ
9   Pool
10 Garage

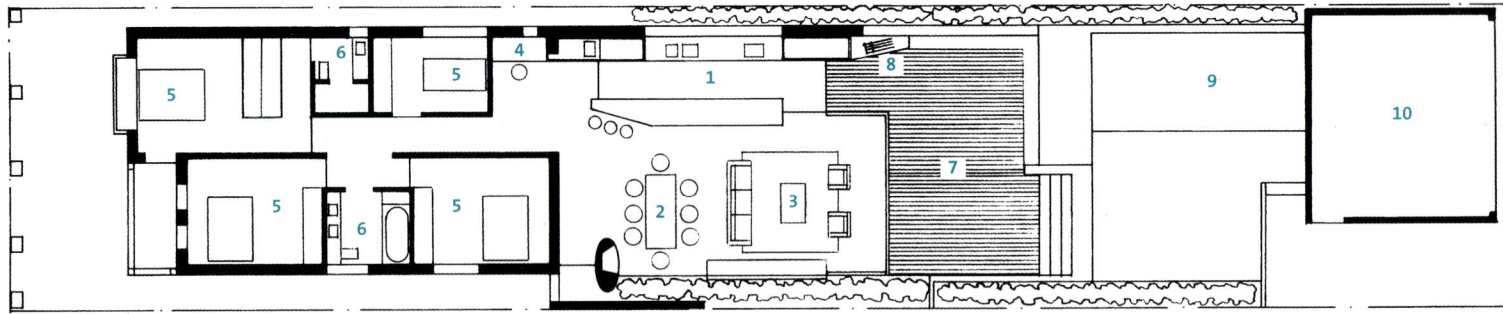

Ground floor

0   5m

Red Hill House

Red Hill, Queensland, Australia

Owen and Vokes

Photography: Jon Linkins

The Red Hill House project is a reoccupation and extension of an existing timber worker's cottage on a steep suburban site. The undercroft of the original cottage has been built in with a series of new living spaces, including a deck that presides over a private garden and the suburb of Red Hill.

The bedrooms for the owners and their two young children are located upstairs, in the original cottage. The character of the worker's cottage is celebrated in the downstairs living spaces. Here the existing floor structure is left exposed and painted white, along with existing and new electrical conduits. Bare light bulbs on electrical flex cord are draped from the existing floor structure to light the new living spaces. Glazed tiling on selected walls reflect the colour of the sky and nearby trees, while bespoke furniture pieces designed specifically for the house facilitate different modes of occupation.

The new eastern facade is tasked with managing both climate and view. The climate is managed by a 700-millimetre framed-cavity wall that is both insulated and ventilated to attenuate the harsh eastern sun in the morning. The view is carefully framed and edited with select openings that optimise outlook while restricting unwanted sun entering the space.

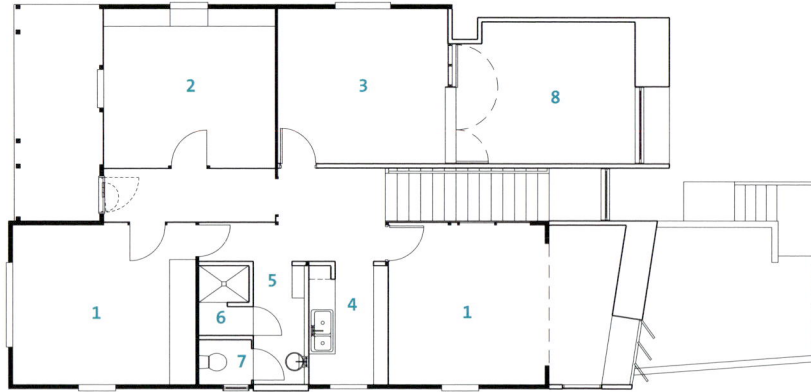

1 Bedroom
2 Home office
3 Nursery
4 Laundry
5 Vanity
6 Shower room
7 Powder room
8 Void to dining room below

First floor

0   5m

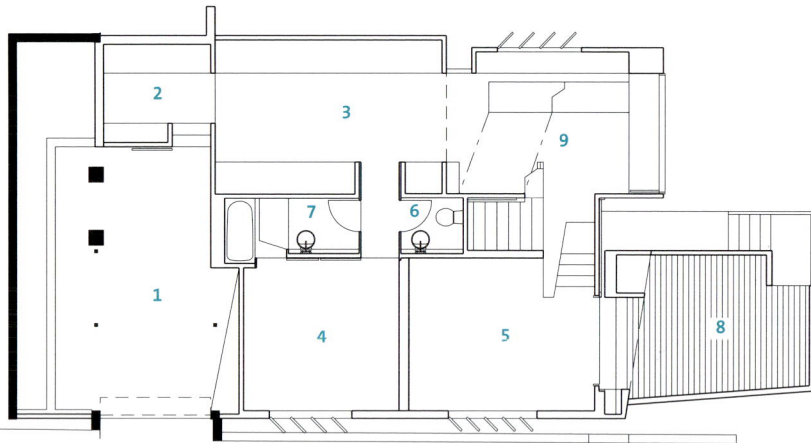

1 Garage
2 Study/Utility/ 'Decompression room'
3 Kitchen
4 Mezzanine
5 Sitting room
6 Powder room
7 Bathroom
8 Deck
9 Dining room

Ground floor

Resort House

Caulfield, Victoria, Australia

Bower Architecture

Photography: Colin Page

Resort House is a project of transformation, where a dark and dilapidated existing suburban house has been converted into a hidden oasis, abundant with natural light and seamlessly integrated indoor and outdoor spaces.

Having bought the existing house for its rear north-facing garden, the owner wanted a series of social living spaces with a resort feel, to be enjoyed with family and friends. The new design simplifies the original plan through the insertion of a high entry gallery, and relocates living areas to the rear (north) across both floor levels. Hi-Light louvre windows surrounding the gallery gently illuminate the owners' art collection with southerly light and encourage natural ventilation so that the entire house can 'breathe'.

At first-floor level (the children's domain), a large cantilevered deck overhangs the alfresco area and is connected to the pool via an external spiral stair. Extensive operable glazing to the northern facade, and the continuous flow of timber, concrete, stone and marble, further strengthen the focus toward the garden and pool, dissolving boundaries between building and landscape.

The resulting house is one rich in possibilities and joy, enveloping its inhabitants in a sunny, social sanctuary which embraces the surroundings and thrives in the Australian climate.

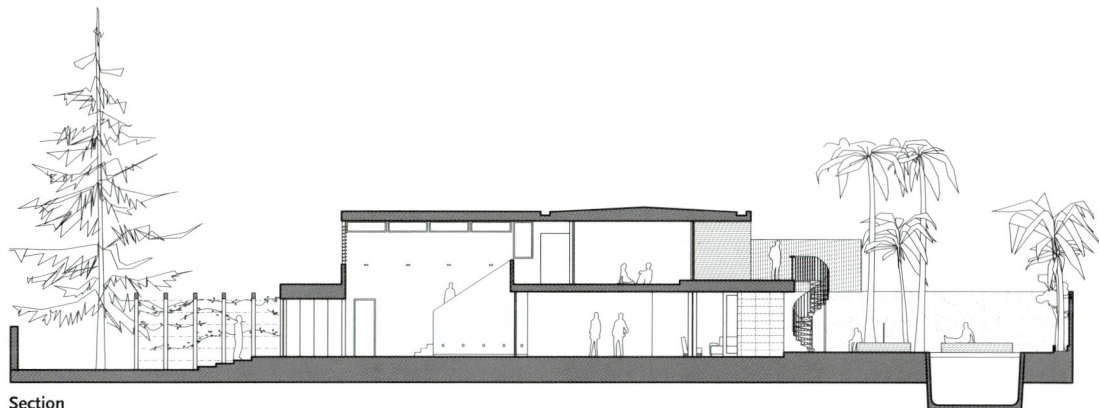

Section

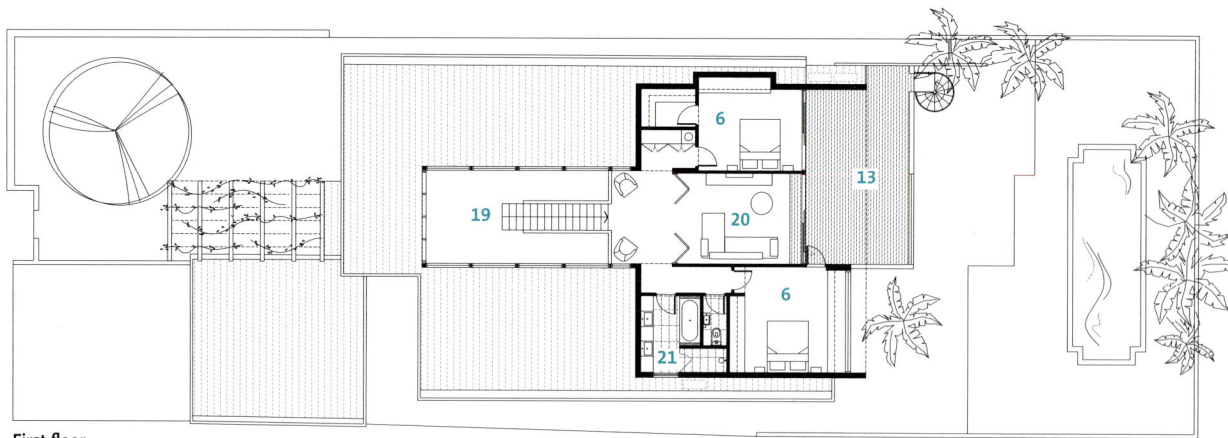

First floor

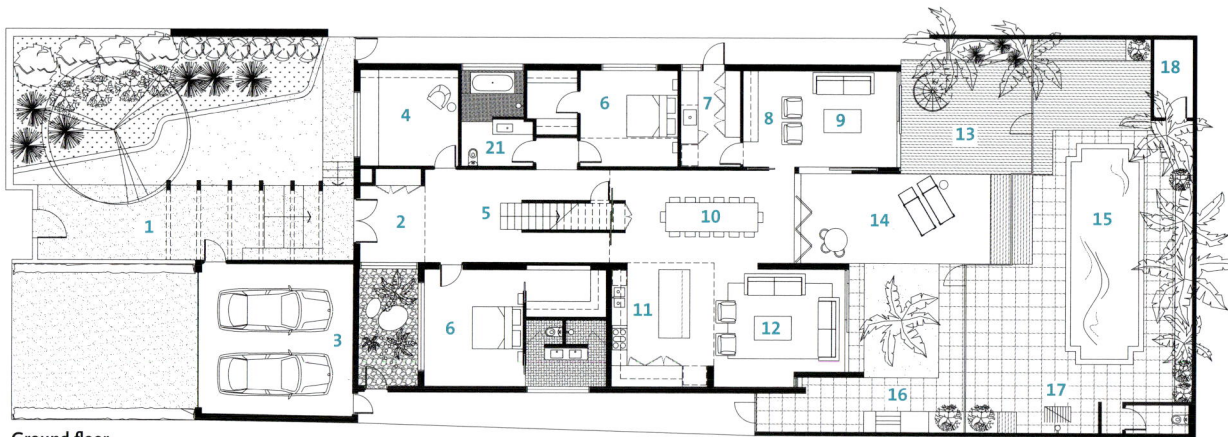

Ground floor

0   5m

1   Entry arbor
2   Entry
3   Garage
4   Study
5   Gallery
6   Bedroom
7   Laundry
8   Bar
9   Lounge
10   Dining room
11   Kitchen
12   Living room
13   Deck
14   Outdoor dining area
15   Pool
16   BBQ
17   Outdoor shower
18   Shed
19   Void
20   Rumpus room
21   Bathroom

Richmond Remodel

Richmond, Victoria, Australia

Ed Ewers Architecture

Photography: Ed Ewers Architecture and Greg Sims Photography

This inner-city remodel is an exploration of contemporary architecture (behind a respectfully restored heritage front), responsible sustainable initiatives, and deceptively large accommodation within a building area of 190 square metres.

The main requirements of the client's brief were to respect the old cottage but provide a modern open-plan addition, keep a generous (for Richmond) garden with direct access to the kitchen, and be environmentally responsible.

The addition faces west, so controlling heat gain from the west was paramount—windows were tinted, external blinds were integral, window openings were kept to a responsible size, and deciduous trees were kept.

Pragmatic materials were used on the first floor (Colorbond wall cladding to blind sides, and compressed fibre cement sheeting to the cranked face), to avoid costly/difficult maintenance, whereas the ground level is clad with ship-lap cypress timber to provide a warm, tactile material which connects with the garden.

The design takes a simple 'box' form and cranks planes to give movement and interest, showing just what can happen when you take an 1880s cottage, remove the 1970s lean-to, and add a young family with an open mind and a bit of cool.

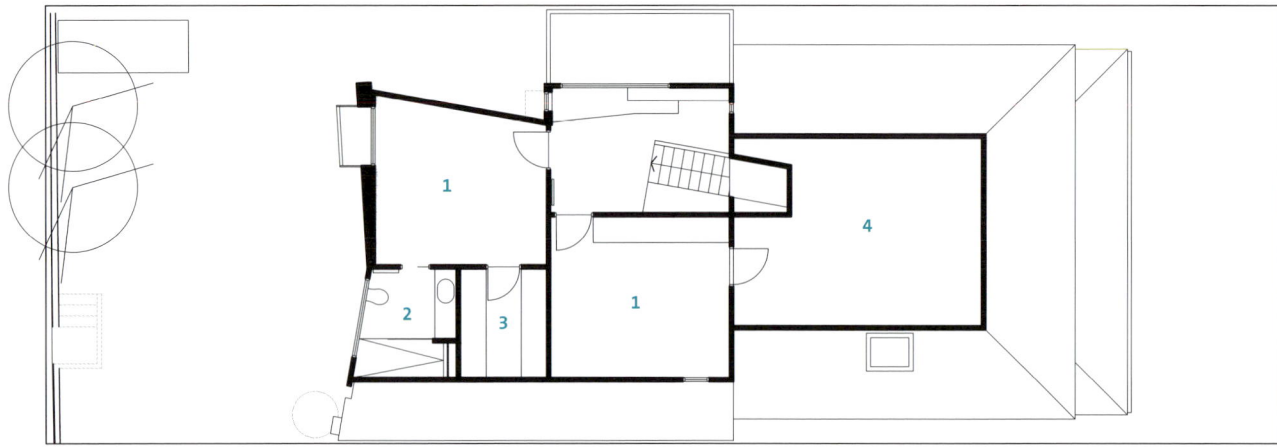

1 Bedroom
2 Ensuite
3 Walk-in-robe
4 Store room

First floor

0   5m

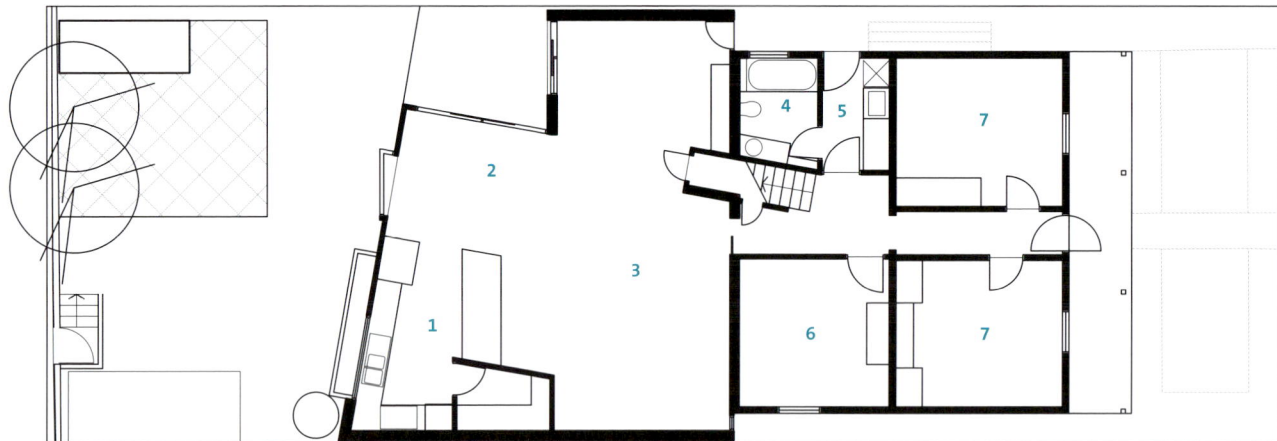

1 Kitchen
2 Dining room
3 Lounge
4 Bathroom
5 Laundry
6 Study
7 Bedroom

Ground floor

Samford House

Samford, Queensland, Australia

Bligh Graham Architects

Photography: Jon Linkins

This house is situated on a modest 600-square-metre block located at the edge of a semi-rural village, overlooking the adjoining bush reserve. The design plays on the notion of the house being on the edge or transition between the city and the country, with rendered walls (city) overlapped by the timber and zinc envelope (bush). This overlap of city and bush is reinforced by the layering of hanging gardens and vine trellises, which further blur the building into the bushland backdrop.

The simple palette of external materials is echoed in the interior. While the exterior is robust in nature, the interior is warm and rich with a reticence suitable for the housing of a large artwork collection.

The L-shaped plan of the house creates a north–east facing courtyard—a hidden 'walled garden'. The principal spaces of the house are constructed as the threshold between the miniature landscape of the courtyard garden and the expanse of the bushland beyond. Large windows and doors disappear so as to seamlessly connect the inside to outside—simultaneously intimate and grand.

The house also incorporates many environmentally-friendly design elements, such as a natural cooling process in which air is drawn into the 'coolth store' of the basement level and up through the central atrium to exhaust out of the high-level clerestory windows.

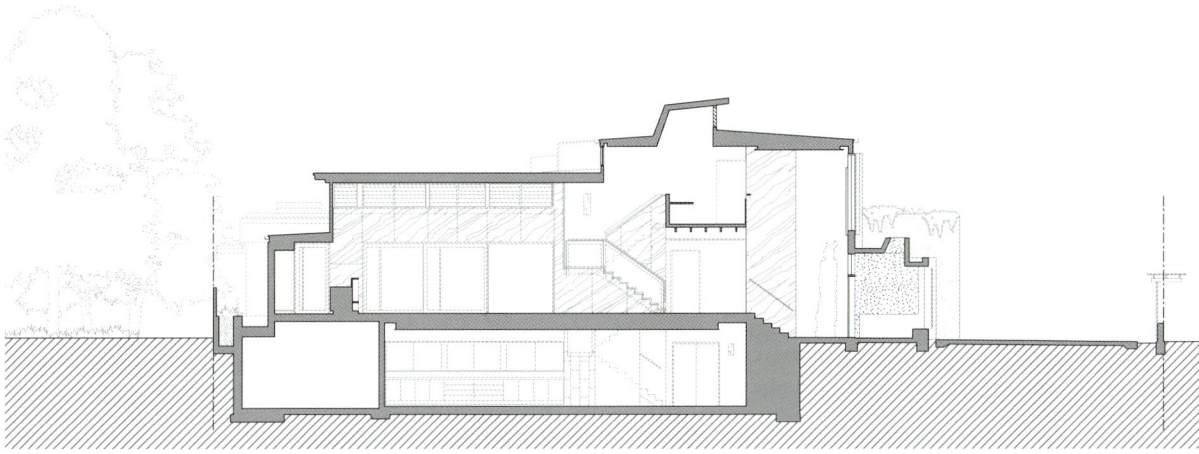

Section

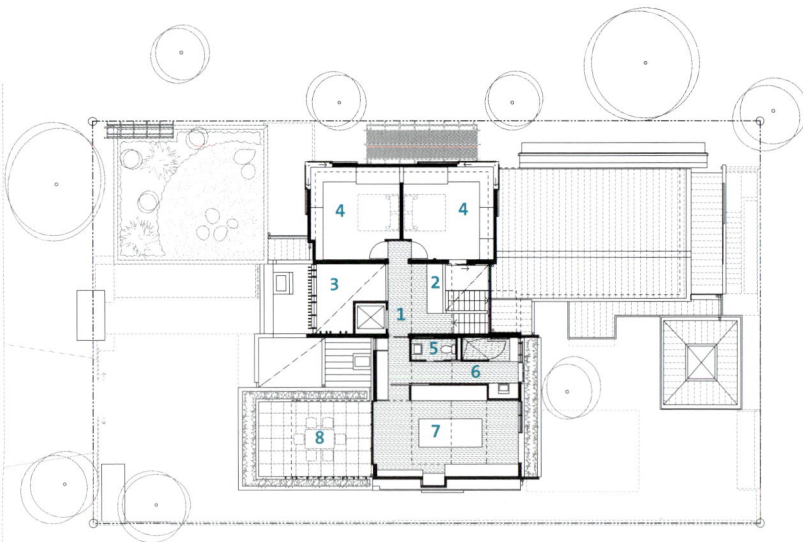

First floor

1 Lift
2 Bridge/Study
3 Void
4 Bedroom
5 Powder room
6 Bathroom
7 Craft room
8 Terrace

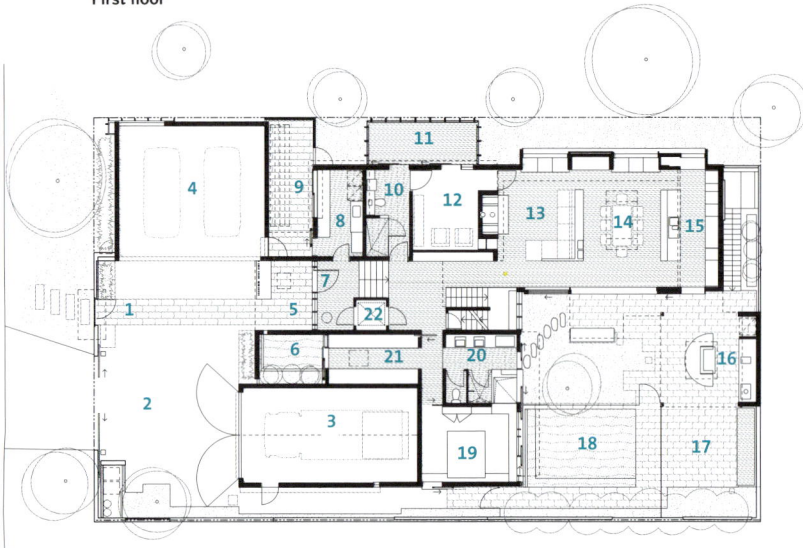

Ground floor

1	Gatehouse	12	Guest bedroom
2	Driveway	13	Living room
3	Motor home	14	Dining room
4	Garage	15	Kitchen
5	Porch	16	Outdoor kitchen
6	Pond	17	Pool terrace
7	Entry	18	Pool
8	Laundry	19	Master bedroom
9	Drying court	20	Ensuite
10	Guest bathroom	21	Walk-in-robe
11	Screened deck	22	Lift

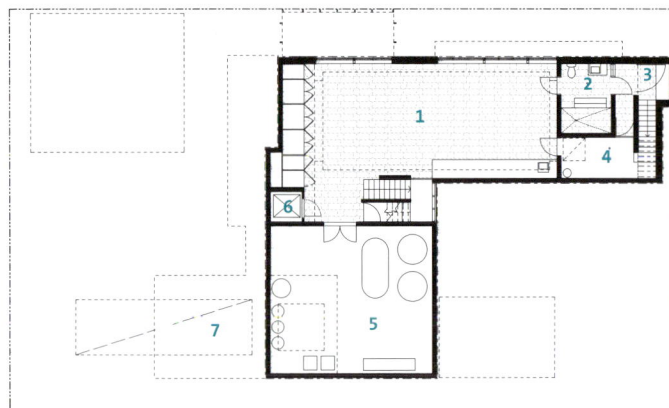

Basement

1 Client's retreat
2 Change room
3 Access to pool
4 Pool plant
5 Plant room
6 Lift
7 Water tank below garage

0 ⸻ 6m

Scarp House

Castlecrag, NSW, Australia

Kooi-Ying Architects

Photography: Eric Sierens

With Scarp House, the aim was to create a calming sanctuary to which the owners could return and snuggle up inside.

Located on the foreshore within the Griffin Conservation Area of Castlecrag, a harbourside suburb of Sydney, the house stays true to Griffin's version of houses nestled within the bush among the sandstone-rock outcrops. Here, public and private spaces merge, and the boundary between them dissolves.

Environmental restraints prevented the new structure from extending much beyond the existing footprint, with the result that a new contemporary house had to flourish within that envelope.

The site posed difficulties, with huge rock outcrops inclining steeply to the rear of the property. However, this was transformed into an opportunity to bring nature inside and make it the focus of the interior experience—an approach started by Frank Lloyd Wright and given expression here by emphatically embracing a prominent rock outcrop as a spectacular central interior feature of the house.

The house is a series of stepped linked volumes immersed in its bush site to avoid interference with the landscape. Visitors to the house first encounter a small glass pavilion punching through the roof, serving as the fifth elevation. As one descends, the living spaces, delightful terraces and bushland dramatically unfold as the new structure negotiates the steep topography of the site.

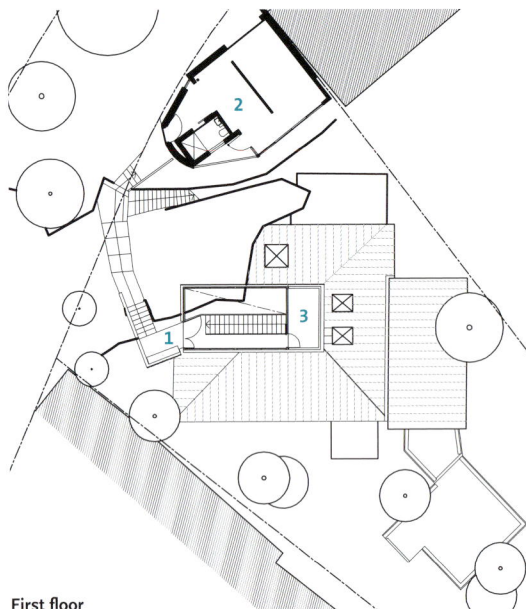

First floor

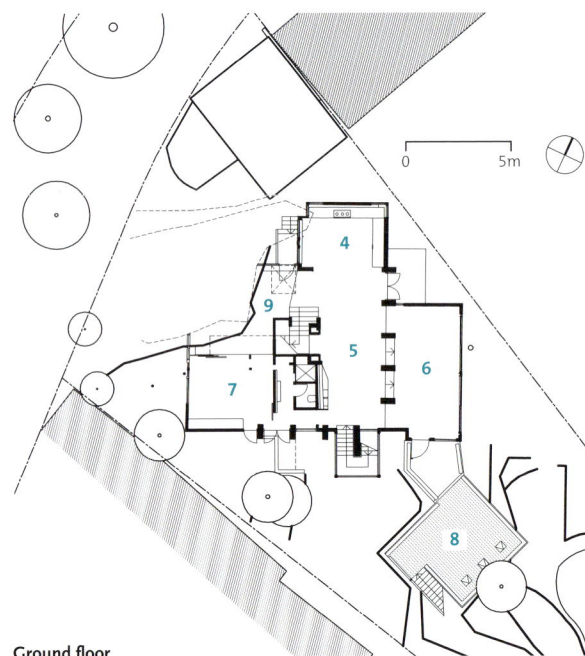

Ground floor

0 ___ 5m

1 Entrance
2 Garage/studio
3 Balcony
4 Kitchen
5 Dining room
6 Lounge
7 Bedroom
8 Terrace
9 Interior rock feature

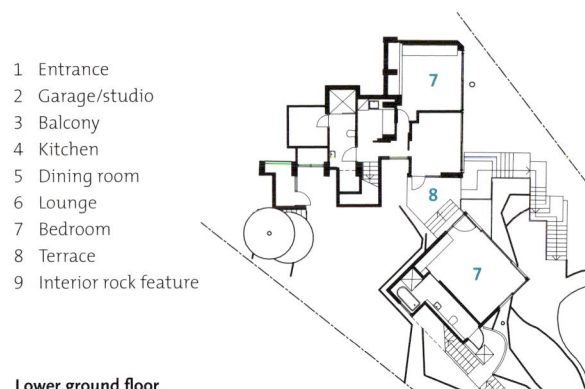

Lower ground floor

202

Simpson Residence

Ascot, Queensland, Australia

Reddog Architects

Photography: Jon Linkins

The Simpson Residence is a reinterpretation of an existing pre-1946 Queenslander, giving new meaning to an old house. Previous adhoc additions were demolished and the building was raised to allow for the integration of three new organisational zones based on a hierarchy of privacy. The existing house now contains the master bedroom, study and a guest bedroom. The upper level of the new north-eastern-facing extension contains living and dining spaces, while the ground level contains private bedroom and secondary family spaces.

The design seeks to respond to the challenges of creating adaptive and flexible spaces for a young family of six. Areas in which the family can play, gather, sleep, work and live have been created, with a particular emphasis on providing opportunities for the family to connect with one another.

The site lies in a distinctive residential urban typology, emphasised by the traditional blocks with detached houses. The architectural proposition responds to the existing typology by forming a contextually sympathetic design proposal that adopts a notion of contrast between old and new elements. The timber and tin of the existing house fronts onto the street, and the new extension to the rear and undercroft adopts a framework in which existing forms, scales and typologies are echoed, but not mimicked. The design seeks to resonate the history of the building instead of merely copying a style.

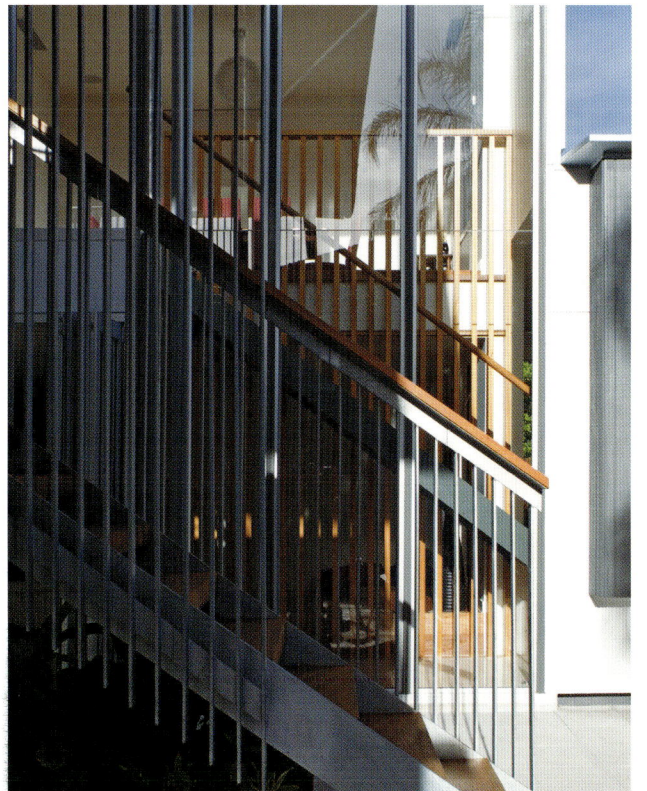

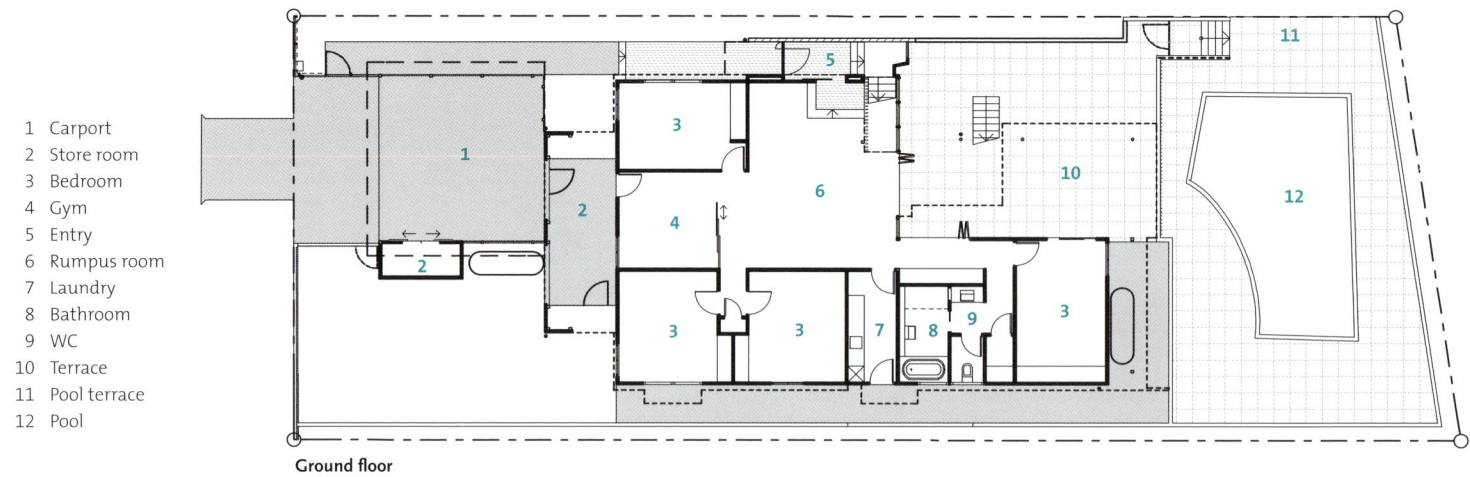

1 Carport
2 Store room
3 Bedroom
4 Gym
5 Entry
6 Rumpus room
7 Laundry
8 Bathroom
9 WC
10 Terrace
11 Pool terrace
12 Pool

Ground floor

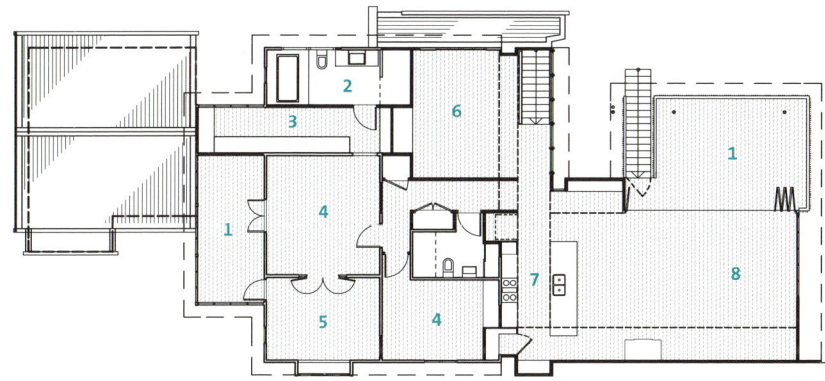

First floor

1 Deck
2 Ensuite
3 Walk-in-robe
4 Bedroom
5 Study
6 Dining room
7 Kitchen
8 Living room

0   3m

Stirling Street

Redfern, NSW, Australia

Mac-Interactive Architects

Photography: Murray Fredericks

This project presented an opportunity to revisit the terraced house typology, which in recent years has been going through extensive reassessment, as terraced houses are turned on their heads to connect the living area (previously a formal room at the front of a terrace) with the rear yard. The kitchen has now become the central focus of a less formal contemporary house.

The client's brief was clear—they did not want a white box minimalist house; nor did they want a house that dictated the style under which they should live.

The timber cladding to the exterior is a direct homage to the derelict weatherboard cottage that previously sat on the site. To maximise the ceiling heights and achieve three storeys, the site was excavated— which determined the need for a concrete slab and upturn walls—which were then expressed rather than dressed.

To avoid a 'white box' and ensure the ground floor did not feel like a 'tube' of living spaces, the living room and dining/kitchen area are separated by a joinery form that wraps around the staircase.

Timber flooring leads upstairs to the 'softer' side of the house—which culminates in a carpeted rumpus/play space in what would have been the attic in a traditional terrace. This space remains connected to the rest of the house by being a mezzanine/loft configuration.

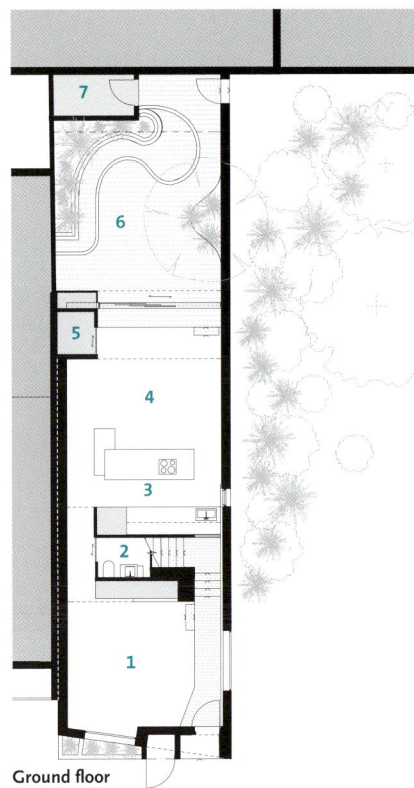
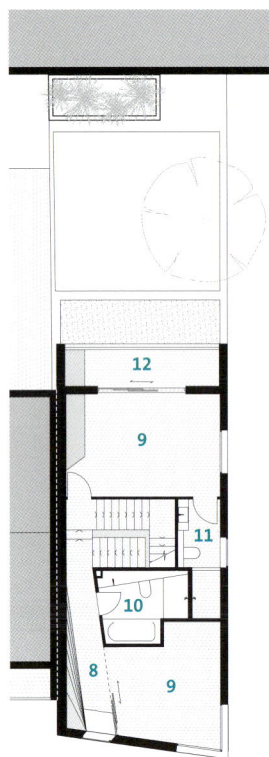
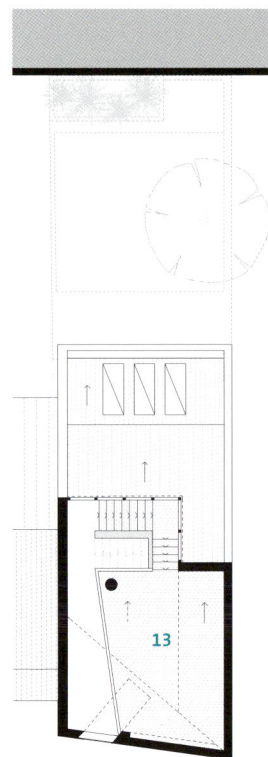

1 Living room
2 Powder room/Laundry
3 Kitchen
4 Dining room
5 Store room
6 Courtyard
7 Garden store
8 Study
9 Bedroom
10 Bathroom
11 Ensuite
12 Balcony
13 Rumpus room

0   4m

Ground floor

First floor

Second floor

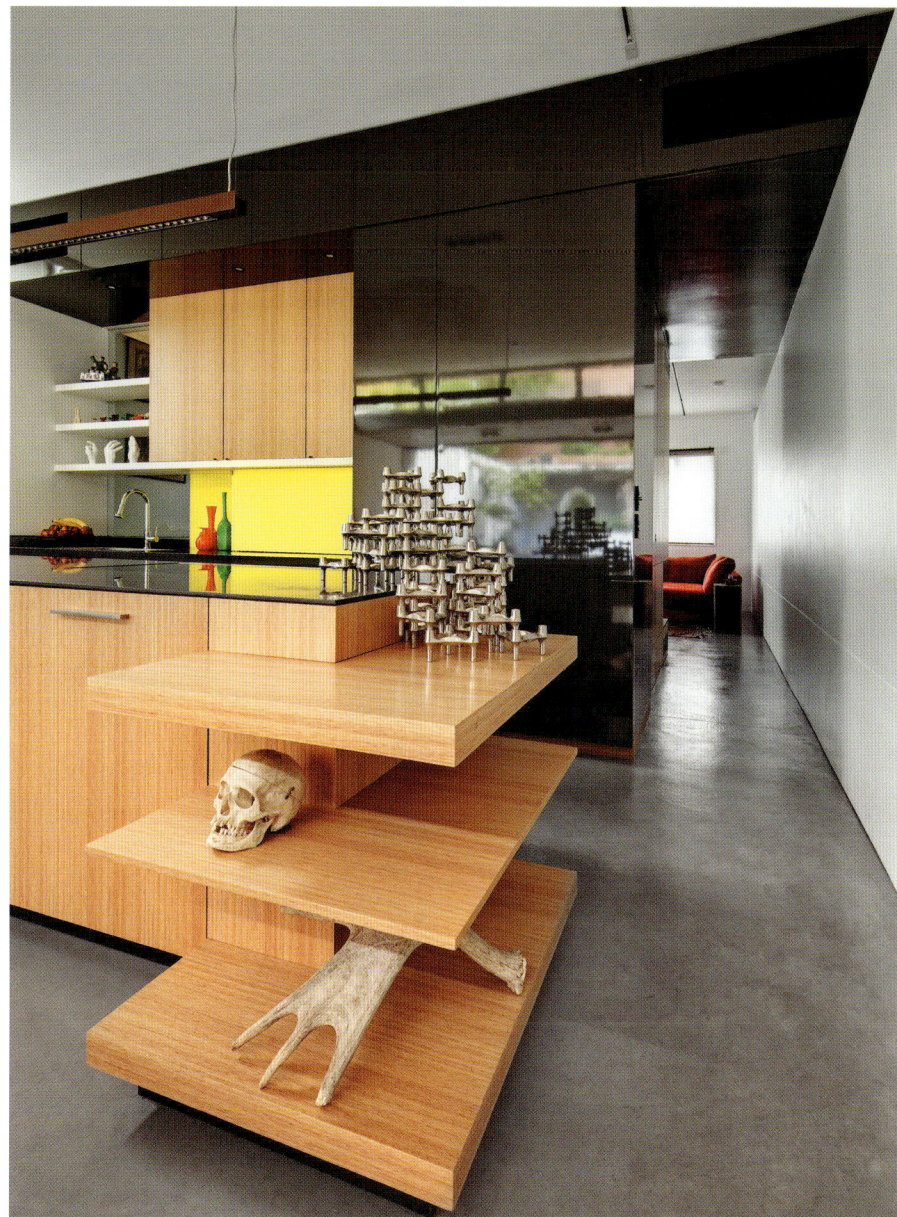

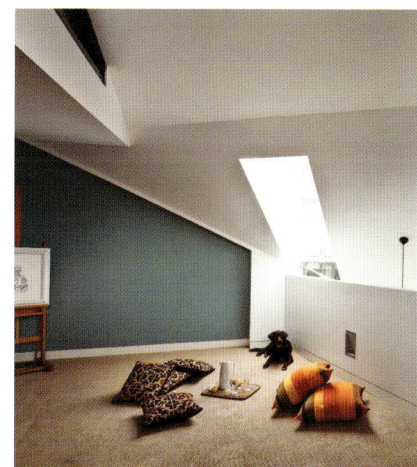

Tattoo House

Fitzroy North, Victoria, Australia

Andrew Maynard Architects

Photography: Peter Bennetts

The Tattoo House project is a small extension to an existing three-bedroom house. The client's brief was delightfully loose—provide new living and kitchen space for a growing young family and create an open plan with plenty of natural light and high ceilings. A kitchen and a flexible work space incorporated into the extension rounded out the brief.

The tight budget generated many of the design decisions. The form is a simple box—the strongest form an architect can achieve at a bargain-basement price. From this starting point, the architect began to express the addition as a covered external space. As the original house is very internalised, the extension was to be as open as possible to create the feel of entering a covered deck rather than an additional internalised space when crossing the threshold between the original and the new structure.

Generally the architect tries to avoid having separate ideas performing different functions and to be economic with concepts so that a couple of key ideas achieve multiple and varied tasks. Every element within the Tattoo House needed to perform multiple functions for maximum return—hence the kitchen bench becomes part of the stair, and the screening, which is required by council, reflects heat and glare away from the expansive windows.

The tattoo motif was conceived as a continuation of the tree graphic around the simple white box to soften the impact of this modern addition to a resolutely 19th-century neighbourhood.

1 Bedroom
2 Living room
3 Dining room
4 Kitchen
5 Deck
6 Bathroom

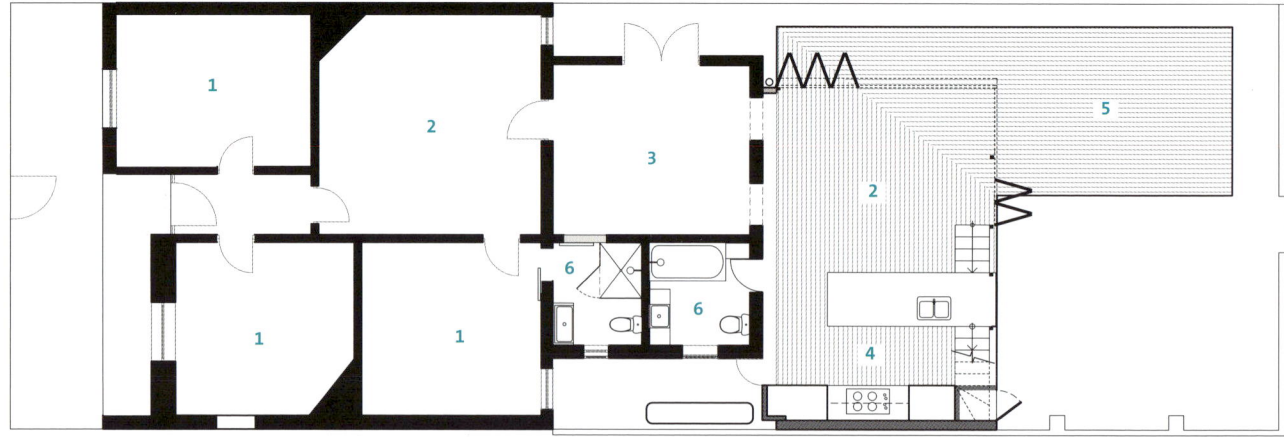

New floor

1 Bedroom
2 Living room
3 Dining room
4 Bathroom
5 Laundry
6 Kitchen
7 WC

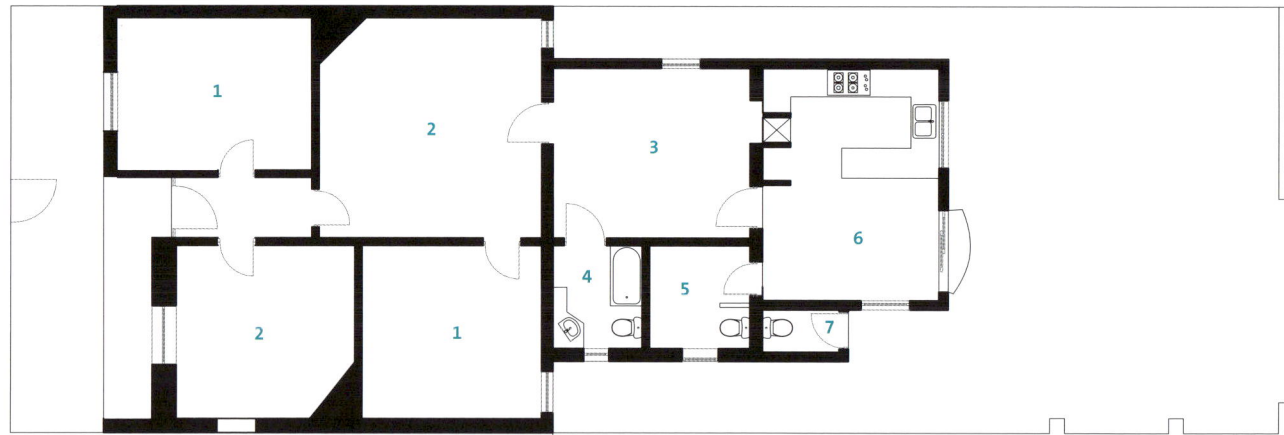

Original floor

0   3m

Te Mata House

Hawkes Bay, North Island, New Zealand

Stevens Lawson Architects

Photography: Mark Smith

Te Mata House sits on a promontory at the foothills of Te Mata Peak, overlooking Hawkes Bay. The clients had run a sheep station at Poranghau for many years and were looking to establish a new home at Te Mata. The architectural response was to create a contemporary home that was infused with a sense of the region and the owners' personal history.

The design comprises three elongated wool-shed forms laid askew across the site and connected by wedge-shaped gallery spaces, creating forced perspective views into the landscape. A series of triangular skylights echo the rocky outcrops on the peak above, capturing the morning sunlight. Two courtyards, a motor court and a central courtyard, are hollowed from the shed forms to create an interlocking sequence of indoor and outdoor spaces. Rough black-stained timber boards are combined with natural timber joinery, polished concrete and rusting steel walls to create an earthy integrity.

The robust rural quality of the exterior gives way to an atmosphere of tranquility and lightness in the interior. There is a particular focus on the framing of specific views into the landscape and the harnessing of natural light throughout the day. The intention was to create an architecture that is both formally and spatially innovative yet deeply rooted in place and history. The house, although highly tuned to the landscape, also acts as a stage that dramatises daily life.

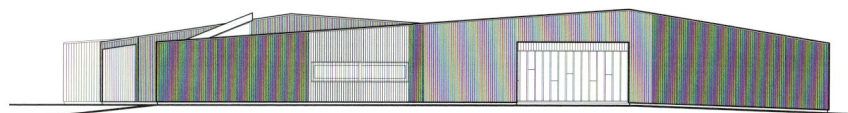

South elevation

1 Deck
2 Kitchen
3 Dining room
4 Living room
5 Garden
6 Lounge
7 Courtyard
8 Hall
9 WC
10 Bedroom
11 Ensuite
12 Dressing room
13 Laundry
14 Office
15 Collections room
16 Wine cellar
17 Garage
18 Store room
19 Boiler room
20 Gallery

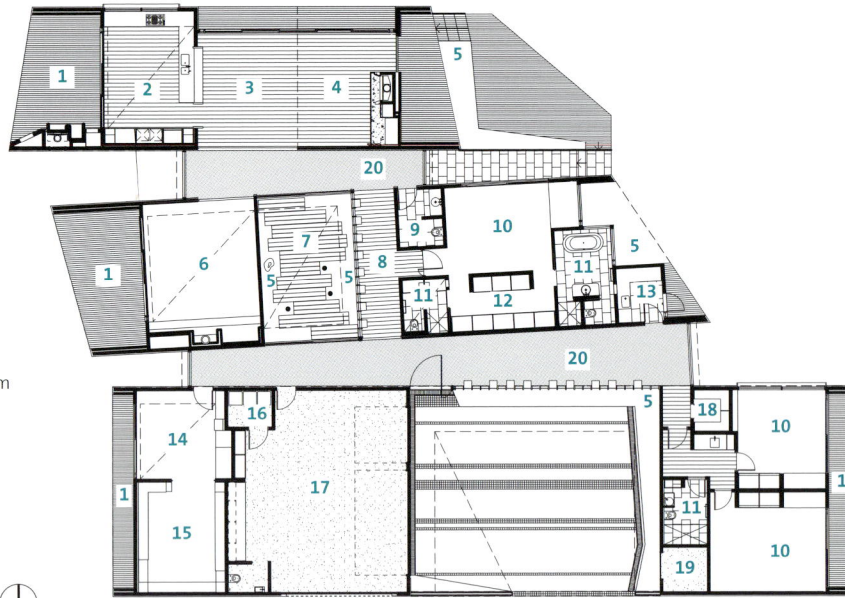

0   5m

Ground floor

Ten Legs House

Geelong West, Victoria, Australia

Ed Ewers Architecture

Photography: Ed Ewers Architecture and
Aaron Cebo Photography

This renovation forms a modest architectural statement, transcending the suburban vernacular. Its success is most apparent in its spatial qualities, belying the tight footprint of the addition, and in the element of surprise. From the street, only the black door and acrylic door handle suggest any change to the original home. But once inside, the transformation becomes bracingly apparent.

Visitors are led past the original four rooms by a gradually widening passage that opens into the main space, comprising open-plan living with mezzanine over the kitchen. The orthogonal plan 'shifts' to accentuate a series of angles, both in plan and elevation. These shifts are accentuated in the fenestration, mezzanine, external cladding, landscaping and pool.

Built to a tight budget, the concept was conceived from a simple 'form-follows-function' plan, in which subtle planar shifts, choice of materials and method of construction dictated the outcome. Materials were generally selected to be 'installed finished', to limit the number of trades and hence costs.

The north-facing extension was modelled to capture winter sun and reduce summer heat ingress. This is supported by 13,500-litre rainwater tanks, water recycling, double-glazing, superior thermal insulation, and a solar hot-water system. All hardwood salvaged during demolition was collected for firewood.

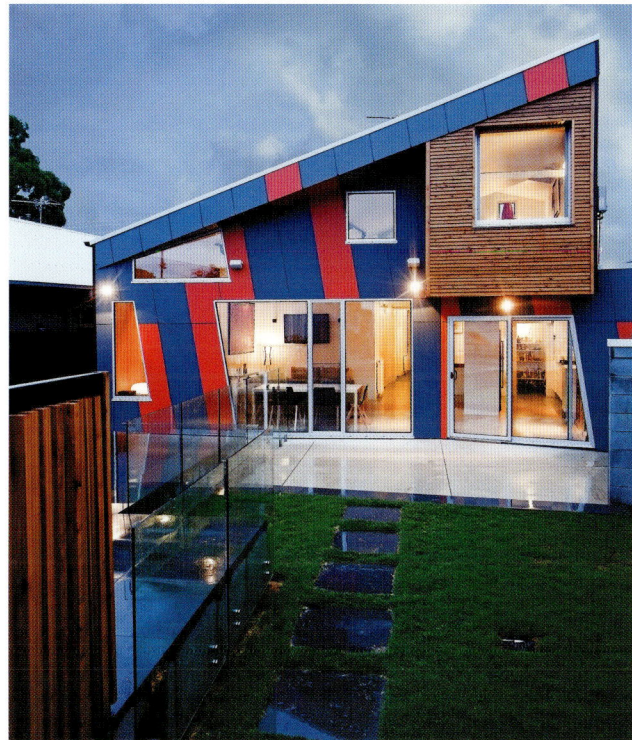

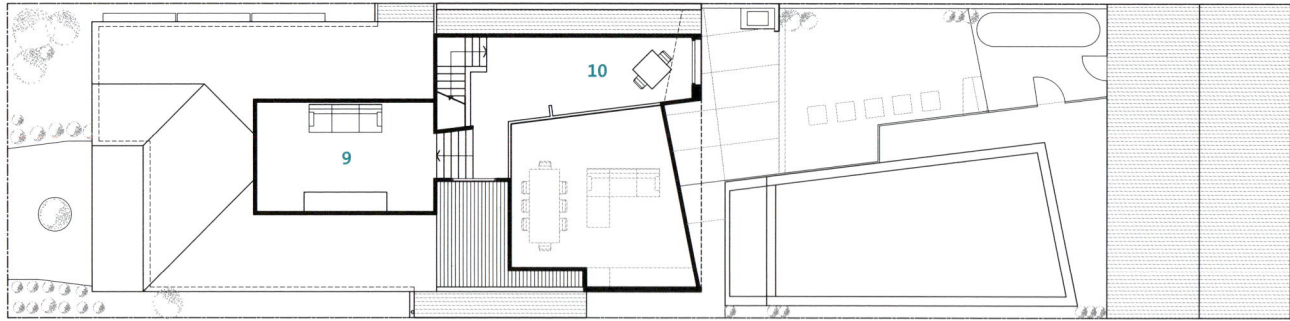

First floor

1 Bedroom
2 Entry
3 Bathroom
4 Kitchen
5 Dining room
6 Living room
7 Laundry
8 Pool
9 Play area
10 Study

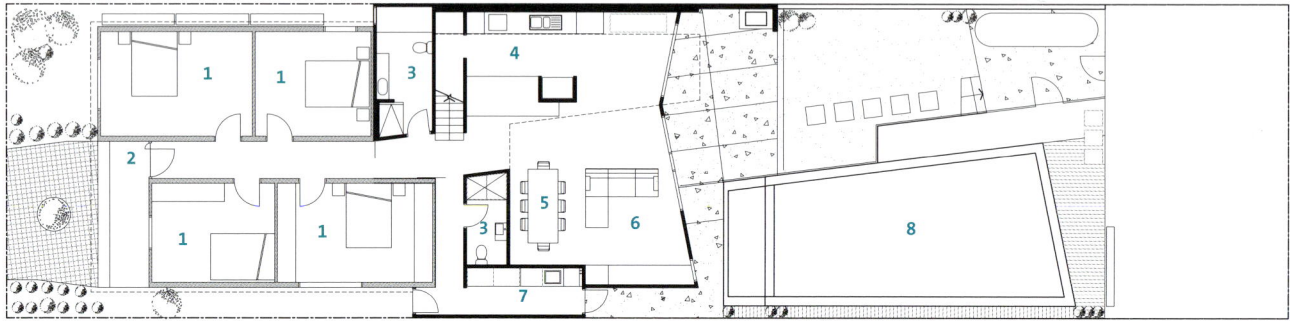

Ground floor

0   4m

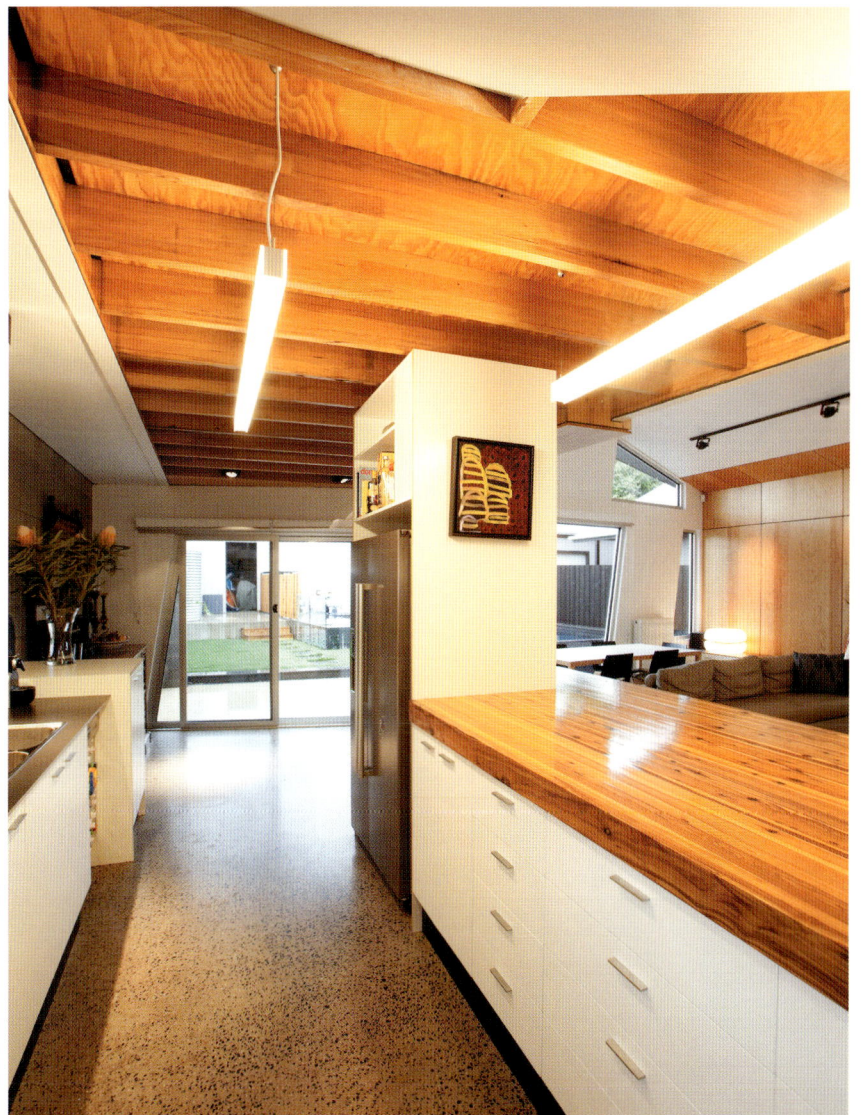

Treloar House

Toowong, Queensland, Australia

Arkhefield

Photography: Scott Burrows
(Aperture Photography)

The aspiration behind the design of Treloar House was to preserve the language and character of the Queenslander while maximising the lifestyle opportunities within the confines of the small site.

The basic program was to lift the original cottage and convert the upper level into the dining room, study and guest suite. The new extension to the rear accommodates the primary living/entertainment areas, with the master bedroom sharing the common outdoor living area. On the ground-floor level, the program is almost duplicated, with the exception of an additional bedroom and kitchenette. The nexus of the house, occupying the junction between new and old, is the large contemporary kitchen (on the upper level), offset by the original VJ walls and ceiling cladding.

The living space seamlessly spills out onto a large deck through tall sliding timber and glass doors. The original sleep-out was transformed into the main stair, now framed in hardwood studs which reference the original structure. The stair is clad in translucent sheeting, enabling light to penetrate deep into the belly of the house while offering an animated counterpoint between new and old. The kitchen also takes advantage of this light-well, with a stainless steel and glass cooking box punching into the stair void. The original dilapidated French doors to the front veranda were removed and replaced by an operable timber and glass wall, enabling the dining space to engage with the street.

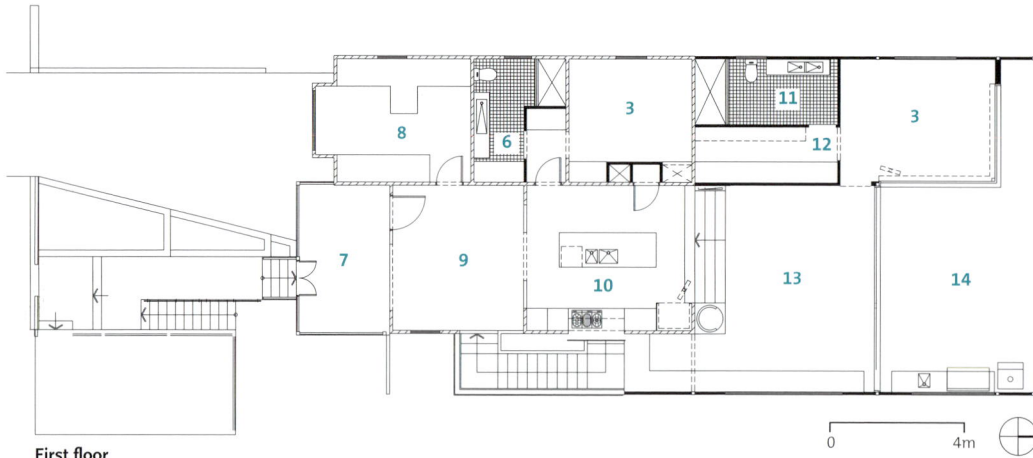

First floor

1 Entry
2 Garage
3 Bedroom
4 Bar
5 Living room
6 WC
7 Deck
8 Study
9 Dining room
10 Kitchen
11 Ensuite
12 Walk-in-robe
13 Living room
14 Outdoor living area

0   4m

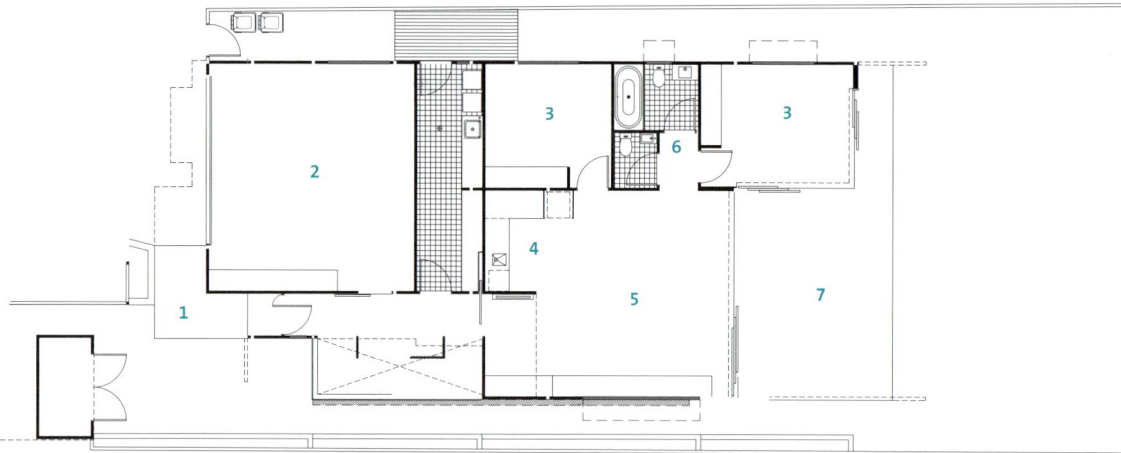

Ground floor

Turn Point Lodge

Pelorus Sound, South Island, New Zealand

Tennent + Brown Architects

Photography: Paul McCredie

The clients were struck by the outlook and drama of a narrow ridge facing northwest and overlooking gullies full of Nikau and the long reach of the Pelorus Sound. The challenge of this site was accessibility, for both materials and labour. It was decided to adopt the strategy of heli-lifting nearly pre-finished buildings and sub-floor frames to the site to minimise the need for site labour. The brief called for two separate private spaces and a communal building that sits parallel to the sound below. The living pavilion extends out at each end, providing morning and evening outdoor spaces. These spaces receive sun and shelter from the land and sea breezes. Attention was given to the spaces between the buildings with terraces and decking, and the retention of existing trees. External louvres and shutters close down the steel boxes when unoccupied. Solar panels with a back-up generator power the lodge.

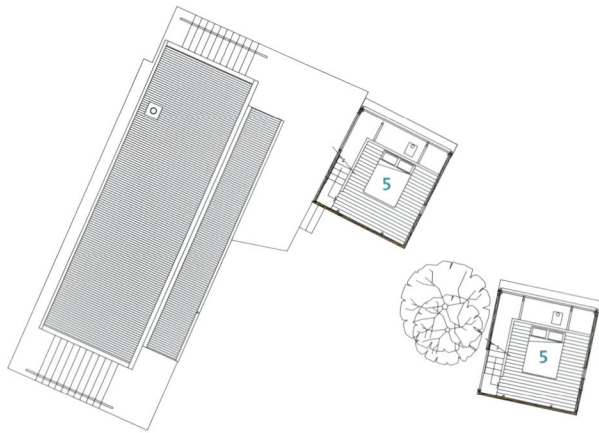

First floor

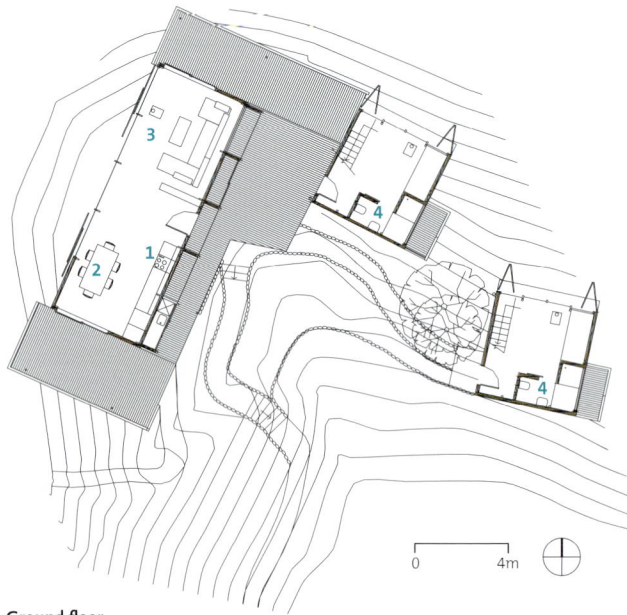

Ground floor

0   4m

1 Kitchen
2 Dining room
3 Living room
4 Bathroom
5 Bedroom

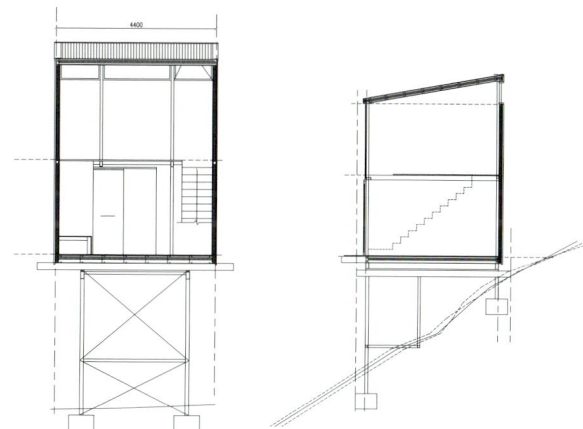

Turramurra House

Turramurra, NSW, Australia

Cullinan Ivanov Partnership

Photography: Charmaine Pang

The original house had been 'renovated' badly by the previous owner. The existing stair made circulation in the house very awkward, its location creating a large area of 'dead' space. The existing windows and walls limited both solar access to the space and blocked desired views.

The resulting renovation introduces a new stair and bathroom, a new kitchen/laundry to the north and three steel boxes, which punch through the southern wall to provide a connection to the existing trees and landscape. The steel boxes, constructed with 10-millimetre mild steel sheets measure 2.4 metres high by 2 metres wide by 1.2

metres deep. They contain a series of joinery units, which are painted in a fluorescent green to further enhance the connection with the outside vegetation.

The new stair, made with 10-millimetre steel folded plate, has a resin finish to the threads. The stair rests on a concrete plinth, which continues to create a day bed to the eastern corner of the living room area. The central core of the stair is clad in a rich dark timber veneer, which balances the starkness of the steel.

The kitchen is raised above the main floor by a step, and the floor treatment changes from timber to white resin flooring.

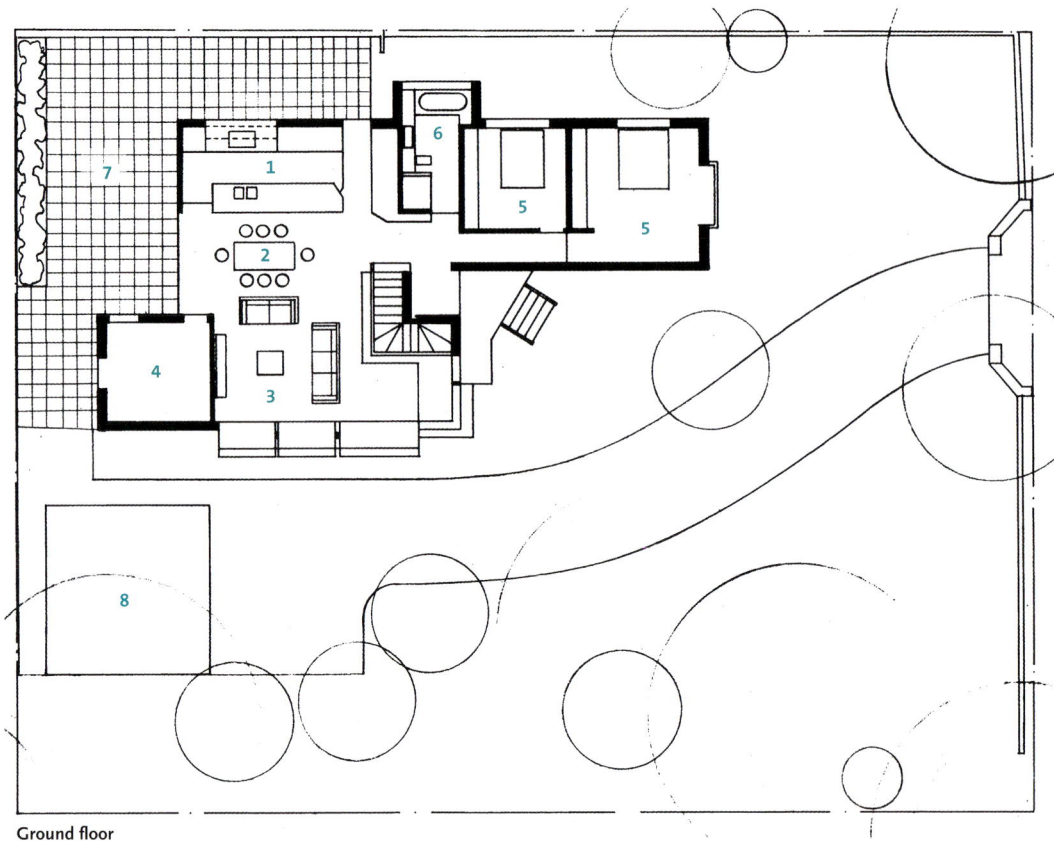

Ground floor

1 Kitchen
2 Dining room
3 Living room
4 Study
5 Bedroom
6 Bathroom
7 Deck
8 Garage

0   4m

Turramurra Park House

Turramurra, NSW, Australia

Liquid Architecture

Photography: Willem Rethmeier

The existing dwelling was a single-storey 1960s brick bungalow elevated above the street, with a cramped plan that under-utilised the opportunities of the sloping site. The clients therefore desired to rework and extend the existing floor plan to create a spacious, open-plan family home with a strong connection to the site and its landscaping. A unique contemporary aesthetic was desired, integrating their own collection of paintings, furniture and objects collected from South-East Asia.

The existing ground floor was simplified to clarify the spatial flow and frame views both internally and to the backyard. The new entry stairs are veiled from the street via a freestanding timber screen panel, creating a transitional indoor/outdoor space folding in towards the main entrance. A second storey was added to maximise the opportunities for living space on the ground floor, with voids connecting the levels visually and spatially, through which skylights channel light into the centre of the home. Bold colour is used to link spaces and enliven the interior, while a new outdoor entertainment area and pool connect the indoor and outdoor spaces. Material is also used to delineate and articulate the composition of volumes in conjunction with the horizontal and vertical elements.

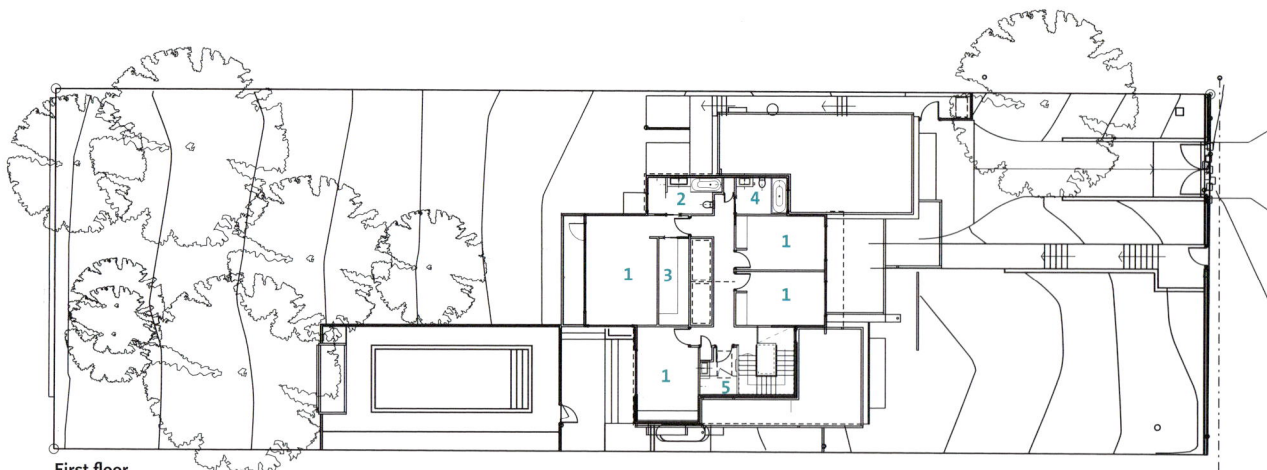

First floor

1　Bedroom
2　Ensuite
3　Walk-in-robe
4　Bathroom
5　Shower room

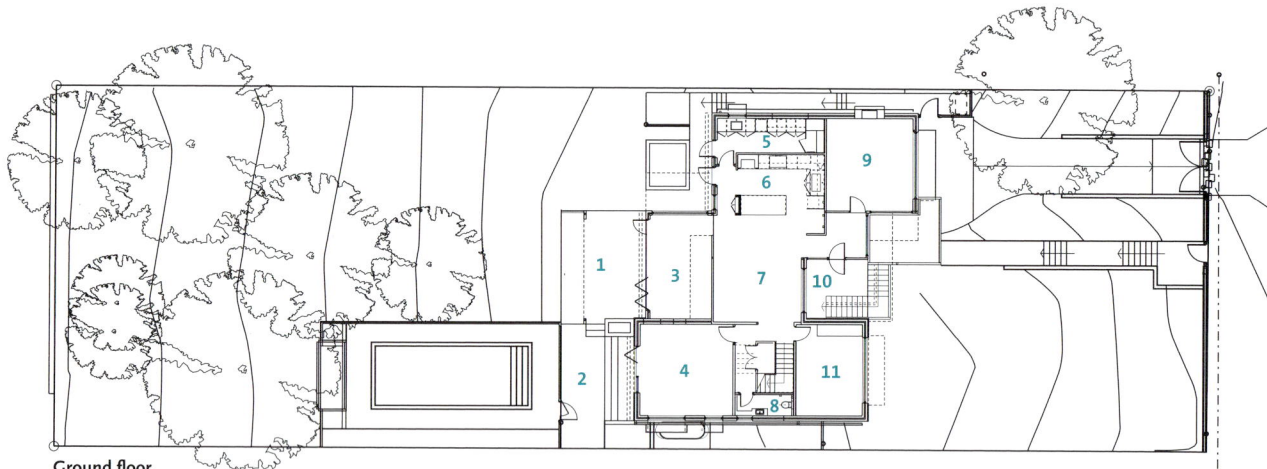

Ground floor

1　Patio
2　Pool patio
3　Dining room
4　Rumpus room
5　Laundry
6　Kitchen
7　Family room
8　Powder room
9　Lounge
10　Entry
11　Study

0　　　　　　10m

Vader House

Fitzroy, Victoria, Australia

Andrew Maynard Architects

Photography: Peter Bennetts

Emerging from behind its high boundary wall, the distorted roof form of Vader House interrupts the symmetrical roof line typical of Fitzroy, and breathes new life into this Victorian terrace.

The eastern and western facades of the extensions are encased in a shield of louvres, which peel back to reveal a folded internal environment of soft colours framed by exposed steel beams. Splashes of deep red playfully enliven the interior, which is occasionally punctured by windows allowing a cinematic light to dance over the internal workings of the Vader House.

The refined material and colourful palette used in the extension, wrapped in a heavy roof form, distinguishes it from the dark masonry-clad terrace from which it emerges. These two opposing forms are united by a transparent glass corridor along the northern boundary wall, framing an outdoor courtyard.

Strategic planning located the courtyard at the heart of the site, allowing both the terrace and extension to have direct contact with this outside space. It creates a central 'demilitarised zone' that allows activities from the surrounding living spaces to spill into, ensuring the site is utilised in its entirety.

Definition between these internal and external environments is barely distinguishable. Transparent bi-fold doors allow for constant physical and visual interaction between these environs. The extensions are therefore at once inside and out. The courtyard's location also provides abundant natural light and ventilation into both the terrace and extension, importantly decreasing reliance on mechanical heating and cooling systems.

The open and seemingly simple nature of Vader House later reveals itself to be one of complexity and ambiguity.

1 Living room   6 Trapdoor to cellar
2 Walkway   7 Courtyard
3 Living area   8 Retractable deck
4 Kitchen   9 Carport
5 Bathroom

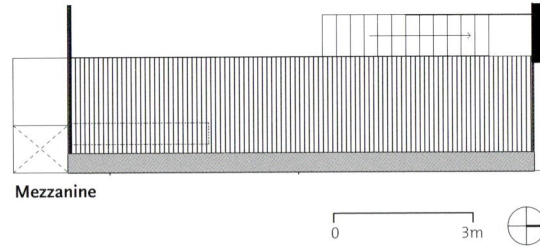

Mezzanine

0   3m

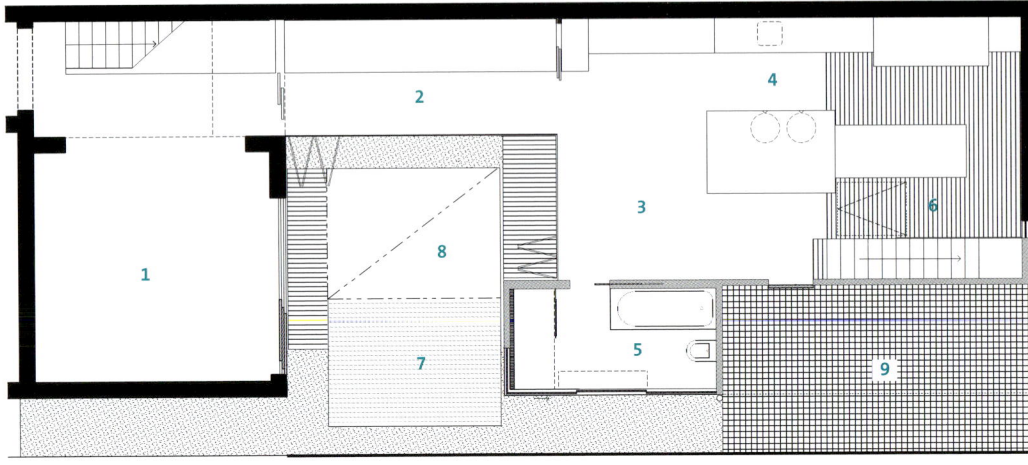

Ground floor

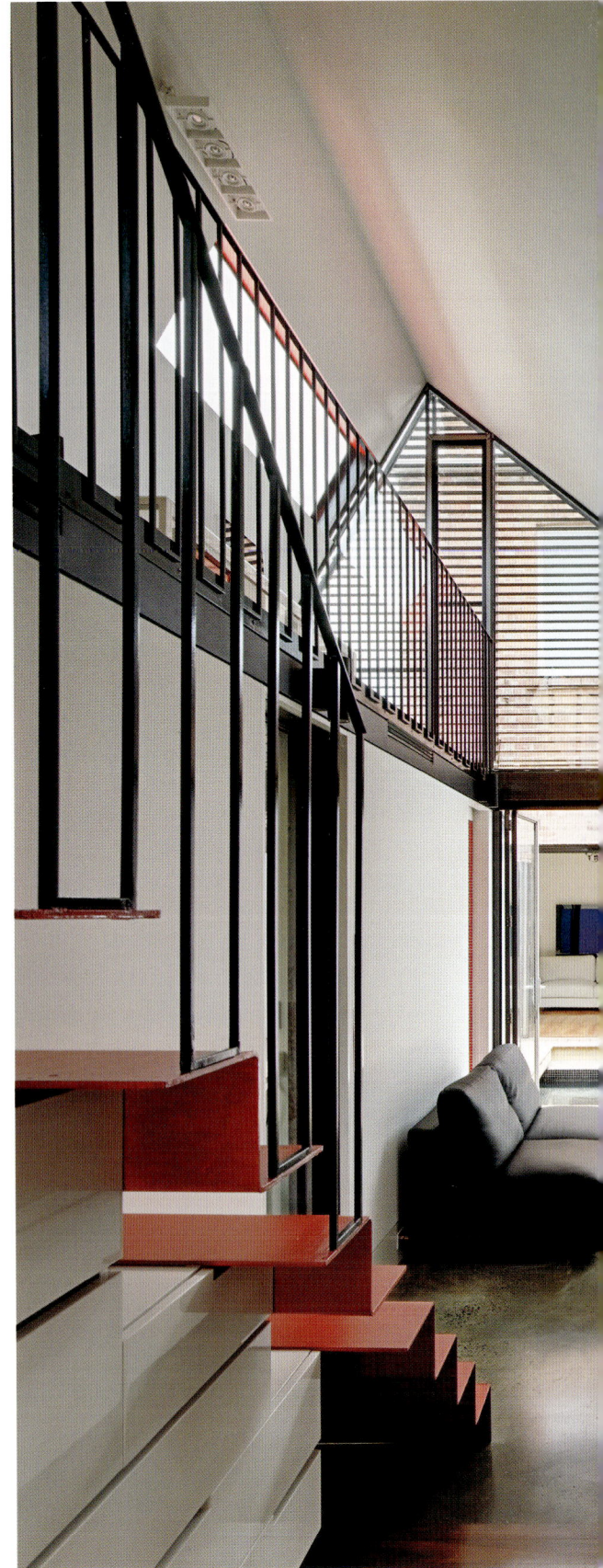

Villiers Street House

Brisbane, Queensland, Australia

Arkhefield Architects with Shaun Lockyer

Photography: Scott Burrows
(Aperture Photography)

The Villiers Street House is an overtly contemporary pavilion/extension to a Queenslander cottage on a typical small lot site in inner-city Brisbane. The choice to build a 'pavilion' to the rear of the existing cottage appeared an obvious one. The challenge was the dilapidated and unspectacular nature of the existing cottage. How to maintain the idea of the cottage and the integrity of its proportion were critical issues.

The design looks to preserve the existing architectural vernacular while offering a challenging juxtaposition with the new built form. This contrast is clearly evident in the application of colour, material and form—the entry sequence through to the front door/stair connection is the junction between old and new.

The language of the house is all about the celebration/interrogation of the Queenslander theme. An 'undercroft' aesthetic, manifest in detail, is explored in both the new and the old, as well as the concept of arrival and definition of edges.

The retention of the old cottage preserves cultural and architectural identity and, more basically, public expectation. The contemporary extension is largely invisible from the street and therefore looks to preserve the character and qualities of this inner-city suburb.

While the house has unquestionably had to address broader needs, the design has allowed the owner to live in a way that maximises the benefits of the benign climate.

Section

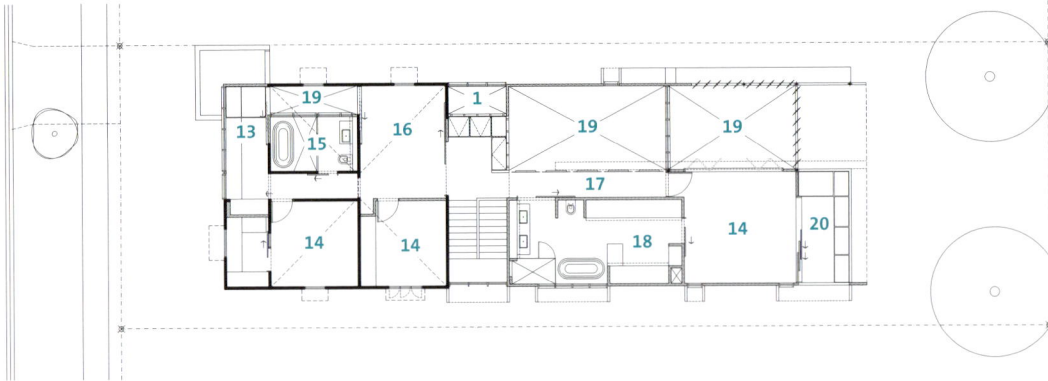

First floor

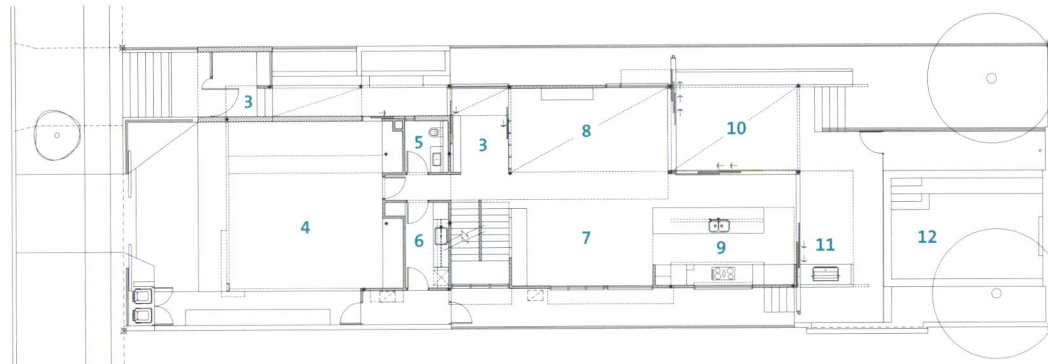

Ground floor

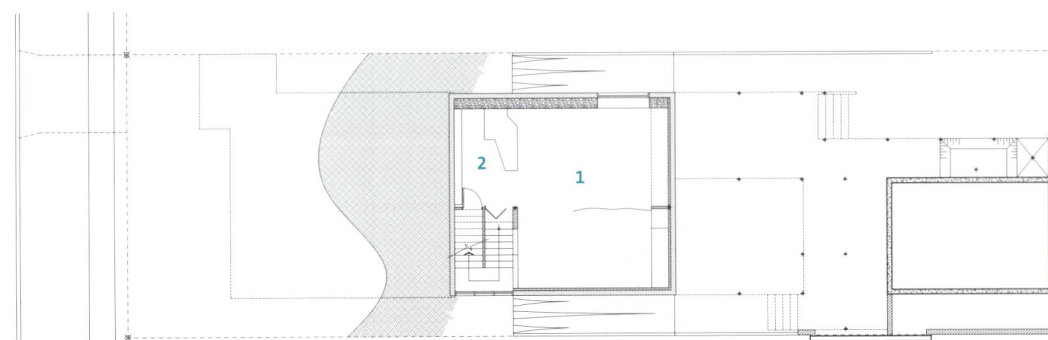

Basement

1   Family room
2   Wine store
3   Entry
4   Garage
5   Powder room
6   Laundry
7   Dining room
8   Living room
9   Kitchen
10 Outdoor living area
11 BBQ
12 Pool
13 Study
14 Bedroom
15 Bathroom
16 Family room
17 Bridge
18 Ensuite and robes
19 Void
20 Deck

0   5m

Wave House

Sydney, NSW, Australia

Sam Crawford Architects

Photography: Brett Boardman

The Wave House constitutes a modest addition to an interwar bungalow. The site is unusual in that it is accessed from a narrow laneway on the fringe of the central business district and falls steeply into a densely vegetated gully overlooking a valley of eucalypts and mountains in the distance. It is in turn overlooked on three sides by multi-storey buildings.

Our brief was to create a new dining/living room, laundry/WC and bathroom. By placing the new spaces on the cramped southern side of the site we avoided compromising the original house and its historic connection to the site. The resultant form ensures privacy from the surrounding buildings while remaining open to the winter sun and expansive views to the west.

The new roof lifts sufficiently over the existing building to provide both winter sun and summer shade. The eastern wall of the folded extrusion is polycarbonate sheet, offering ample light and privacy. The use of inexpensive materials, such as polycarbonate and custom-orb sheeting, bamboo, bare-faced concrete block and cyclone fencing, ensured costs were kept to a minimum.

As architects, the single largest contribution that we can make to environmental sustainability is convincing our clients to retain as much of the existing building fabric as possible, intervening when required to improve thermal and water efficiency, and adding only what is necessary. This project is a simple and effective illustration of how this can be done with delight.

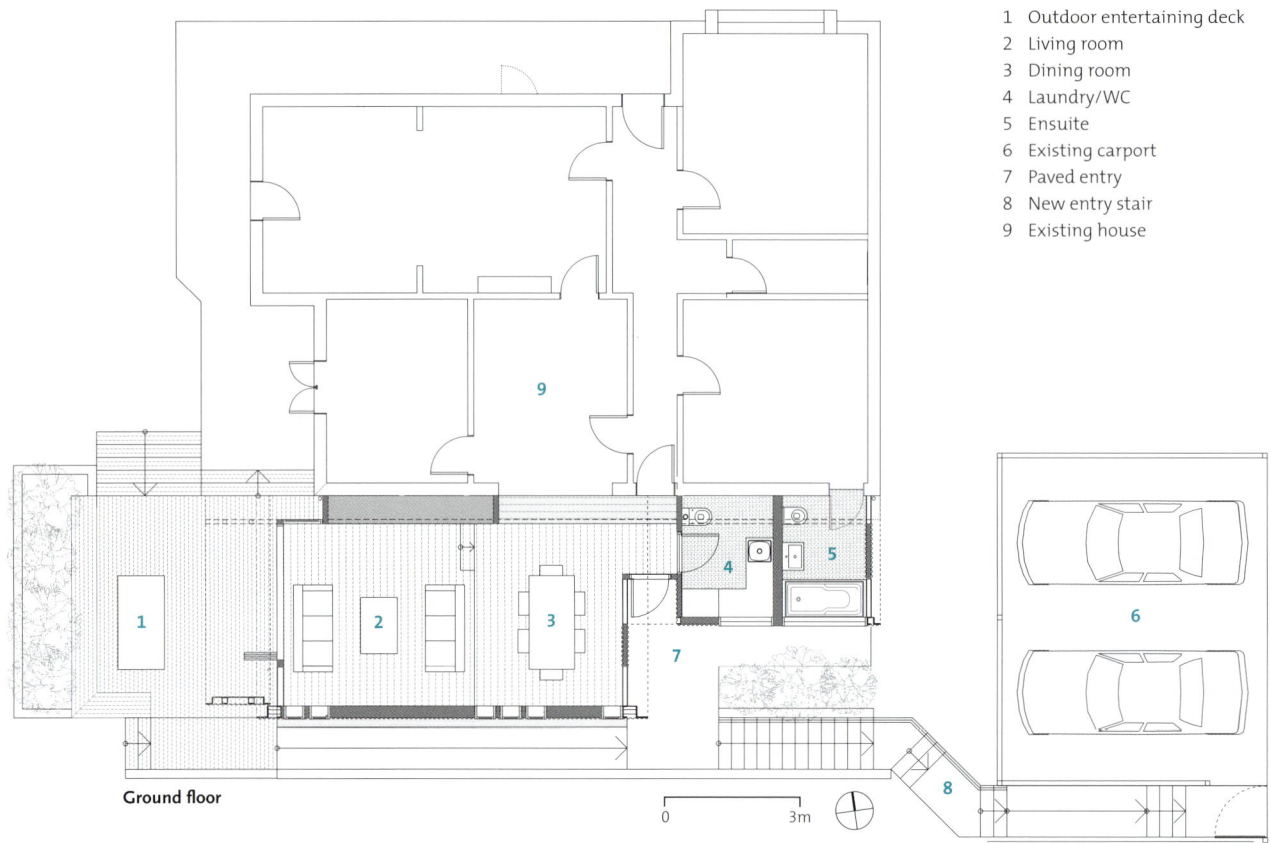

1 Outdoor entertaining deck
2 Living room
3 Dining room
4 Laundry/WC
5 Ensuite
6 Existing carport
7 Paved entry
8 New entry stair
9 Existing house

Ground floor

0   3m

Woollahra House 11

Woollahra, NSW, Australia

Grove Architects

Photography: Willem Rethmeier

Woollahra House 11 is situated in the heart of the heritage conservation precinct of Paddington and Woollahra, on Sydney's urban fringe, opposite a small native park to the north and a recycled neo-gothic sandstone church to the west. There are no vacant sites in this 150-year-old inner suburb, but there are a few buildings, recognised as inappropriate, earmarked for demolition should the occasion arise. This 250-square-metre site represented one of those rare opportunities.

The client, a mature couple, required an individual studio work space each, the usual functional living spaces, and a separate bedroom suite for frequent guests and overnighting grandchildren. At the lower level, with its own independent access, is an elegant yoga teaching studio with ancillary rooms, adjacent to the two-car garage.

The architecture was required to respond functionally, climatically and aesthetically to its extraordinary context and to engage with contemporary sustainability standards. The house won the 2008 Woollahra Conservation Award. In the words of the jury: "The design places itself firmly in the 21st century and forms a reference point to the various architectural styles around. It captures the essence of indoor and outdoor living in an elegant manner, without ostentation and pretence, in the use of subdued materials, minimal furnishings, natural colours and clean lines."

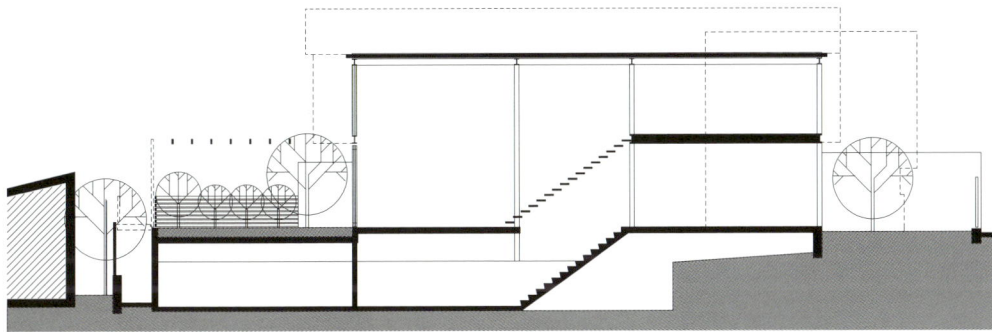

Section

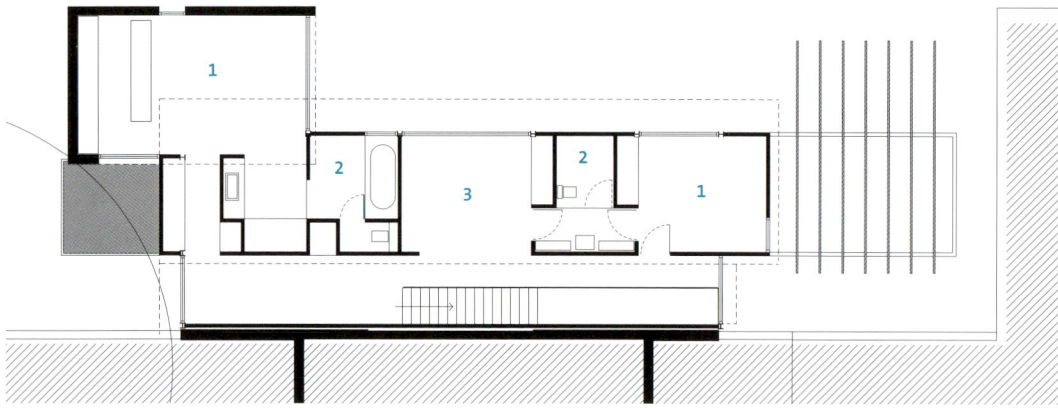

First floor

1　Bedroom
2　Bathroom
3　Office/Bedroom

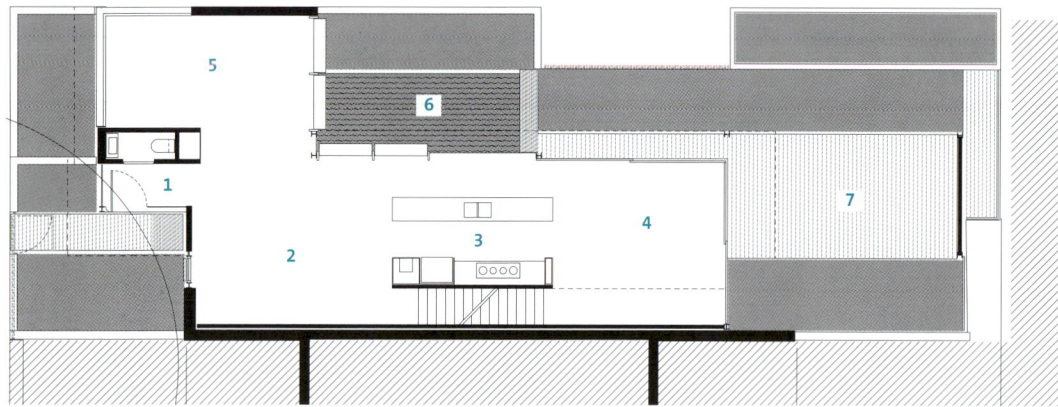

Ground floor

1　Entry	5　Studio
2　Lounge	6　Pond
3　Kitchen	7　Deck
4　Dining room	

Lower ground floor

1　Plant room	4　Studio
2　Laundry	5　Garage
3　Bathroom	

0　　　　5m

Woollahra House 6

Woollahra, NSW, Australia

Grove Architects

Photography: Willem Rethmeier

Woollahra House 6 is part of a small complex of six houses, including an art gallery and café, on an 1800-square-metre triangular-shaped site on a prominent corner in the heart of the heritage conservation precinct of Paddington and Woollahra, on Sydney's urban fringe. While each of the houses is quite different from the next, each shares a contemporary architectural language designed to respond to the broader heritage context.

This three-level house occupies a 300-square-metre sector of the overall site and has two street frontages. It presents three large bedrooms, each with its own facilities; a laundry and a study on the top floor; and a flexible courtyard plan at the main level, with a 12-metre lap pool and an independent studio/office. The lower level provides another independent office, media room, wine cellar, gymnasium and three-car garage.

The entire focus of the house is on the central landscaped courtyard. The main internal rooms, the external dining area and pool, and the remote studio/office all interface with this beautiful garden, making for an oasis of calm and elegance in the urban environment.

The whole complex won a 2004 Woollahra Conservation Award, and a Royal Australian Institute of Architects' Multiple Housing Architecture Award in 2006. The individual house shown here was shortlisted for the Royal Australian Institute of Architects' Single Housing category in the same year.

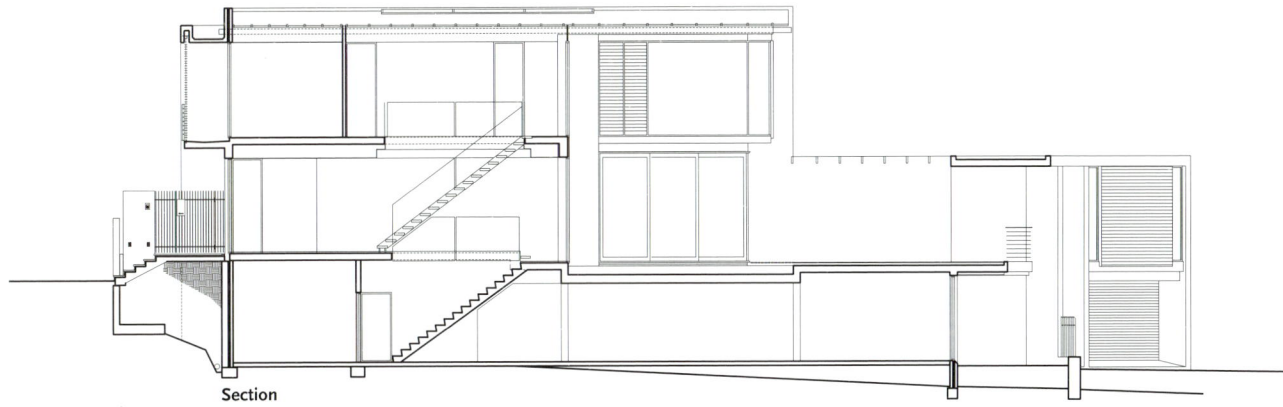

Section

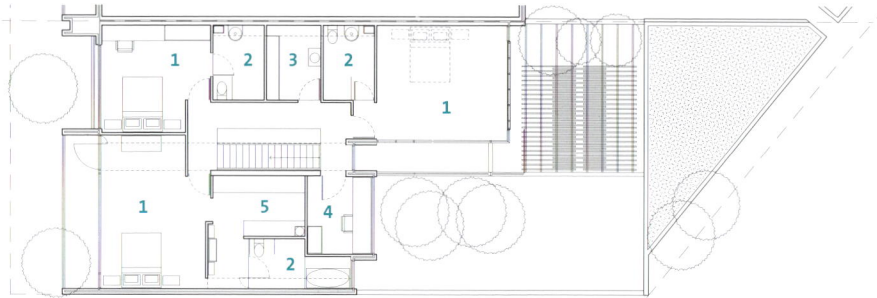

1 Bedroom
2 Bathroom
3 Laundry
4 Study
5 Walk-in-robe

Second floor

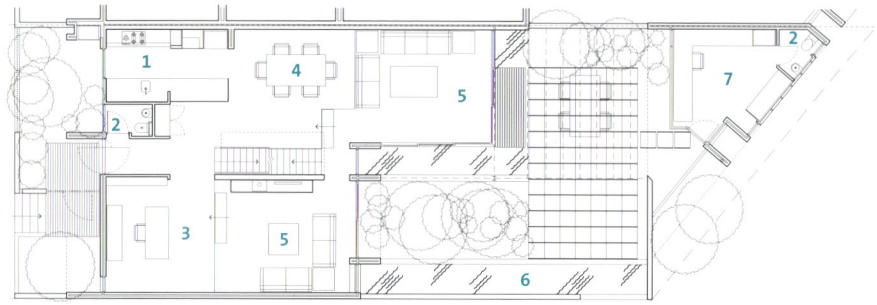

1 Kitchen
2 Bathroom
3 Library/Study
4 Dining room
5 Living room
6 Lap pool
7 Office

First floor

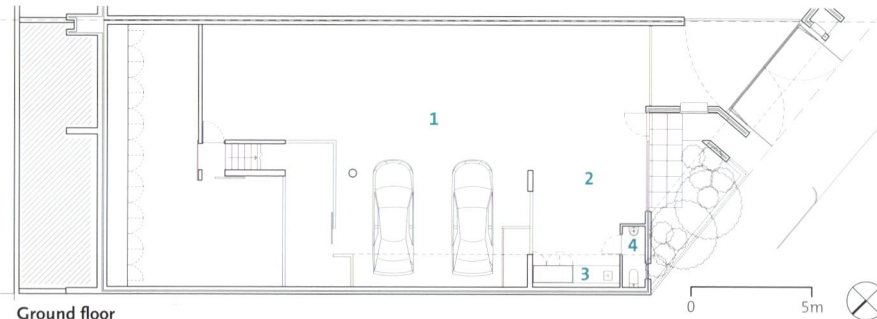

1 Garage
2 Office
3 Kitchen
4 Bathroom

Ground floor

0   5m

Architect contact details

Andrew Maynard Architects Pty Ltd
Suite 12/397 Smith Street
Fitzroy Vic 3065, Australia
+61 3 9939 6323
www.maynardarchitects.com

Arkhefield
418 Adelaide Street
Brisbane Qld 4000, Australia
+61 7 3831 8150
www.arkhefield.com.au

BKK Architects (Black Kosloff Knott Pty Ltd)
Level 9, 180 Russell Street
Melbourne Vic 3000, Australia
+61 3 9671 4555
www.b-k-k.com.au

Bligh Graham Architects
3 Dairy Farm Lane
Cedar Creek Qld 4520, Australia
+61 7 3289 4566
www.blighgraham.com.au

Brian Meyerson Architects Pty Ltd
Level 1, 151 Curlewis Street
Bondi Beach NSW 2026, Australia
+61 2 8284 5777
www.bmarchitecture.com.au

Bower Architecture Pty Ltd
28 King Street
Prahran Vic 3181, Australia
+61 3 9521 2552
www.bowerarchitecture.com.au

BVN Architecture
365 St Paul's Terrace
Fortitude Valley Qld 4006, Australia
+61 7 3852 2525
www.bvn.com.au

Circa 2000 Architecture + Construction
Suite 27 Campus Village
Smithfield Qld 4878, Australia
+61 7 4057 9922
www.circa2000.com.au

Craig Rossetti Architects
28 Gwynne Street
Richmond Vic 3121, Australia
+61 3 9428 4812
www.rossetti.com.au

Cullinan Ivanov Partnership
123 Commonwealth Street
Surry Hills NSW 2010, Australia
+61 2 9212 1796
www.cipartnership.com

Ed Ewers Architecture
6/617–643 Spencer Street
West Melbourne Vic 3003, Australia
+61 3 9326 5366
www.ewersarchitecture.com.au

Grove Architects
PO Box 1148
Woollahra NSW 1350, Australia
Sky: +61 414 803 603
John: +61 417 248 510
www.grovearchitects.com.au

Irving Smith Jack Architects Ltd
Studio 180 Bridge Street, Box 222
Nelson, New Zealand
+64 3 548 1372
www.isjarchitects.co.nz

Kamermans & Co. Architects Ltd
Level 1, 394 Remuera Road
Remuera Auckland 1541, New Zealand
+64 9 524 9585
www.kamermans.co.nz

Kevin Hayes Architects Pty Ltd
46 Berwick Street
Fortitude Valley Qld 4006, Australia
+61 7 3852 3190
www.kharchitects.com

Kooi-Ying Architects
9/501 Glebe Point Road
Glebe NSW 2037, Australia
+61 2 9518 7402
www.kooiying.com

KUD (Kavellaris Urban Design)
53 Victoria Parade
Collingwood Vic 3066, Australia
+61 3 9417 1116
www.kud.com.au

KRA (Kathryn Robson Architecture)
PO Box 1481
St Kilda South Vic 3182, Australia
+61 411 259 258
www.k-r-a.com.au

Liquid Architecture
7/100 Penshurst Street
Willoughby NSW 2068, Australia
+61 2 9958 7950
www.liquidarchitecture.com.au

Mac Interactive Architects
94 Cooper Street
Surry Hills NSW 2010, Australia
+61 2 9212 3800
www.mac-interactive.com

Max Pritchard Architect
PO Box 808
Glenelg SA 5045, Australia
+61 8 8376 2314
www.maxpritchardarchitect.com.au

Michael McKenna Architecture & Interiors
Level 3, 358 Lonsdale Street
Melbourne Vic 3000, Australia
+61 3 9640 0433
www.michaelmckenna.com.au

Nathan Gibson Judd Architecture
Level 1, 29 Lonsdale Street
Braddon ACT 2612, Australia
+61 2 6296 1640
www.gibsonjudd.com.au

Nic Owen Architects
260 Elgin Street
Carlton Vic 3053, Australia
+61 3 9347 1140
www.nicowenarchitects.com.au

Owen and Vokes
Level 3, 119 Melbourne Street
South Brisbane Qld 4101, Australia
+61 7 3846 2044
www.owenandvokes.com

Phorm Architecture + Design
Shop 6/173 Boundary Street
West End Qld 4101, Australia
+61 7 3255 2733
www.phorm.com.au

Preston Lane Architects Pty Ltd
45 Goulburn Street
Hobart Tas 7000, Australia
+61 3 6231 2923
www.prestonlanearchitects.com.au

Push
Level 1, 702 Ann Street
Fortitude Valley Qld 4006, Australia
+61 7 3252 0949
www.push.net.au

Reddog Architects
6 Prospect Street
Fortitude Valley Qld 4006
+61 7 3252 8912
www.reddogarchitects.com

Richard Kirk Architect
13 Manning Street
South Brisbane Qld 4101, Australia
+61 7 3255 2526
www.richardkirkarchitect.com

Sam Crawford Architects
Level 5, 68 Wentworth Avenue
Surry Hills NSW 2010, Australia
+61 2 9280 3555
www.samcrawfordarchitects.com.au

Scott Carpenter Architect
43 Longboard Court
Salt Village NSW 2487, Australia
+61 2 6674 0488
www.scottcarpenterarchitect.com.au

Shaun Lockyer Architects
Lightspace Studio 2
30 Light Street
Fortitude Valley Qld 4006, Australia
www.lockyerarchitects.com.au

Stevens Lawson Architects Ltd
19/75 Parnell Road
Parnell Auckland 1052, New Zealand
+64 9 377 5376
www.stevenslawson.co.nz

Studio 101 Architects
1 Dennys Place
Geelong Vic 3220, Australia
+61 3 5221 9131
www.studio101.com.au

To1 Architecture & Interiors
63 Nickson Street
Surry Hills NSW 2010, Australia
+61 2 9698 0411
www.to1.com.au

Tennent Brown Architects Ltd
Level 6, Hope Gibbons Building
7–11 Dixon Street
Wellington 6141, New Zealand
+64 4 382 9248
www.tennentbrown.co.nz

Tobias Partners
27 Renny Street
Paddington NSW 2021, Australia
+61 2 9361 4800
www.tobiaspartners.com

Photographer contact details

Andrew Ashton
+61 3 9421 4021
+61 419 000 850
www.ashtonphoto.com.au

Brad Newton
+61 407 313 111
www.bradnewton.com.au

Brent Middleton
+61 412 754 400
brent.middleton@open2view.com.au

Brett Boardman
+61 418 210 943
www.brettboardman.com

Camera Obscura
+61 438 443 899
www.cameraobscura.net.au

Charmaine Pang
+61 412 858 877
www.charmainepang.com

Christopher Frederick Jones
+61 405 440 180
www.cfjphoto.com.au

Clare and Papi
+61 7 3358 2919

Colin Page
+61 3 9529 4900
www.colinpage.com

Eric Sierins
www.mdaa.com.au

Giles Westley
+61 414 398 333
www.westley.com.au

Greg Sims
+61 3 9529 4900
www.gregsims.com.au

John-Paul Pochin Photography
+64 3 669 2004
www.moments.co.nz

Jon Linkins
+61 7 3355 0073
www.jonlinkins.com

Jonathan Wherrett
+61 400 462 437
www.jonathanwherrett.com

Justin Alexander
+61 414 365 243
www.justinalexander.com.au

Lisa Cohen
+61 412 206 998
www.lisacohenphotography.com

Mark Smith
+64 21 998 694
www.marksmith.co.nz

Matthew Jensen Photography
+61 3 9523 7711
www.mattjensenphotography.dphoto.com

Murray Fredericks
+61 2 9130 3364
www.murrayfredericks.com.au

Paul McCredie
+64 21 477 617
paulmccredie@paradise.net.nz

Patrick Bingham-Hall
www.patrickbingham-hall.com

Peter Bennetts
+61 412 568 181
www.peterbennetts.com

Rhiannon Slatter
+61 402 914 658
www.rhiannonslatter.com.au

Richard Glover
+61 417 654 815
www.richardglover.com

Sam Noonan
+61 411 878 528
www.samnoonan.com.au

Scott Burrows
Aperture Architectural Photography
+61 413 383 940
www.aperture.com.au

Shannon McGrath
+61 407 330 767
www.shannonmcgrath.com

Trevor Mein
+61 3 9859 5699
www.meinphoto.com

Willem Rethmeier
+61 418 247 319
www.willemrethmeier.com